200 budget meals

hamlyn | **all colour cookbook**

200 budget meals

Sunil Vijayakar

An Hachette Livre UK company
www.hachettelivre.co.uk

First published in Great Britain in 2008 by Hamlyn,
a division of Octopus Publishing Group Ltd
2–4 Heron Quays, London E14 4JP
www.octopusbooks.co.uk

Copyright © Octopus Publishing Group Ltd 2008

Some of the recipes in this book have previously
appeared in the following books published by Hamlyn:
Fab Fast Food by Sunil Vijayakar
30-minute Vegetarian by Joanna Farrow

ISBN: 978-0-600-61821-8

A CIP catalogue record for this book is available
from the British Library

Printed and bound in China

1 2 3 4 5 6 7 8 9 10

Both metric and imperial measurements are given for the
recipes. Use one set of measures only, not a mixture of both.

Standard level spoon measurements are used in all recipes
1 tablespoon = 15 ml
1 teaspoon = 5 ml

Ovens should be preheated to the specified temperature.
If using a fan-assisted oven, follow the manufacturer's
instructions for adjusting the time and temperature.

Eggs should be medium unless otherwise stated. The
Department of Health advises that eggs should not be
consumed raw. This book contains some dishes made with
raw or lightly cooked eggs. It is prudent for more vulnerable
people, such as pregnant and nursing mothers, invalids, the
elderly, babies and young children, to avoid uncooked or
lightly cooked dishes made with eggs.

This book includes dishes made with nuts and nut
derivatives. It is advisable for those with known allergic
reactions to nuts and nut derivatives and those who may
be potentially vulnerable to these allergies, such as pregnant
and nursing mothers, invalids, the elderly, babies and
children, to avoid dishes made with nuts and nut oils. It is
also prudent to check the labels of preprepared ingredients
for the possible inclusion of nut derivatives.

contents

introduction

introduction

Just because you're watching your wallet, that doesn't mean you have to miss out on fabulous food. This sensational collection of recipes has been specially created for busy people who want no-fuss meals made from great ingredients that won't break the bank. There's everything from simple starters and snacks to healthy salads and vegetable dishes, hearty main meals and sumptuous desserts. So, whatever you're in the mood for, even if you're on a budget, there's something here to satisfy and enjoy.

Fabulous food on a budget

The secret of creating really delicious meals every time lies in the choice of ingredients.

If you choose good-quality ingredients, it's very hard to go wrong. And the key point is that quality doesn't have to mean additional expense. If you know where to look and what to look for, it's easy to buy fantastic-tasting ingredients economically. So what's the secret?

Spend more to spend less

Sometimes it's worth spending a little extra on a more expensive ingredient because in the long run you'll end up using less of it. For example, Italian Parmesan cheese or a really well-flavoured Cheddar cheese might be more expensive than a block of cheap mild processed cheese, but the flavour is so rich and intense that you only need to use a small amount. If you are making a cheese sauce, for instance, you would need to use far less of the more expensive cheese to achieve a full-flavoured sauce than you would a mild, tasteless one, so weight for weight and price for price, the Parmesan or Cheddar will work out to be a much better buy.

Choose wisely: meat and poultry

These ingredients can really bump up the cost of your meal, but clever shopping can mean luxurious meals that don't cost the earth. When it comes to inexpensive – and quick – eats, minced meat is always a great choice because it's incredibly versatile as well

8

as very economical and speedy, being perfect for meatballs, kebabs, sauces, curries and bakes, to name but a few options. But there are other cheaps cuts that are good too. Pork is generally a reasonably priced meat and pork leg steaks make a great, lean choice, but even more expensive cuts such as prime fillet steak can be made economical by your choice of dish. For example, take a small piece of expensive beef fillet, slice it very thinly and then stir-fry it with plenty of vegetables and you'll have a memorable meal with delicious meat but for very little cost.

Both poultry and meat can be 'stretched' by bulking them out with other cheaper ingredients such as beans, rice, pasta and noodles, as in Rice Noodles with Lemon Chicken, page 144, and Quick Sausage & Bean Casserole, page 146. And you can cut costs with poultry by buying a whole bird

and jointing it yourself, rather than buying individual portions. Alternatively, you can buy cheaper portions such as thighs and drumsticks in bulk and freeze what you don't need for a later date – they can be cooked in delicious dishes such as Fast Chicken Curry, page 132, and Tandoori Chicken, page 156.

Choose wisely: fish and shellfish
Like meat and poultry, fish and shellfish can be pricey, so be prepared to buy what looks good and is well priced on your fishmonger's slab or on the supermarket counter on the day. Fish and shellfish should usually be eaten on the day you purchase them and must be in excellent condition, so check for fresh-smelling fish with shiny skins, bright eyes and firm flesh. As a general rule, avoid buying fish on a Monday. Fish that often offer especially good value for money include salmon, trout, sardines and mackerel. Although some shellfish and seafood such as fresh crab and lobster are expensive, others – notably mussels and squid – are relatively cheap as well as quick to cook, versatile and delicious.

Buy in season
Fresh fruit and vegetables are at their absolute best when they're in season. Ripe, succulent, sweet and juicy – not only do they taste great but they're available in abundance, so are usually better priced. Out of season

ingredients often have an inferior taste and are invariably more expensive because they are scarce. Also, they have frequently been flown in from far-flung places, which again pushes up the price. It's usually true to say that the less-travelled and fresher an ingredient is, the better it will be, so buying locally grown produce is often a good way of ensuring that it's fresh, which in turn reduces the risk of wastage.

But, whether you're buying in-season or imported produce, make sure that your items of choice look in good condition before purchasing. If fruit and vegetables appear tired and wilted, it's a good rule of thumb to assume that they're past their best, so always choose the freshest-, firmest-looking specimens. If the leaves are attached, they should be green and fresh looking. Don't

worry whether the produce is perfectly round and uniform, but do make sure that it's not bruised, soft or wrinkled.

Opt for fruit and/or vegetable boxes

One of the easiest ways to get healthy, seasonal, good-quality fruit and/or vegetables – and without even having to spend money on transport – is with a box delivery scheme. Check out a local scheme in your area to have locally grown, seasonal fruit and vegetables delivered direct to your door. They offer a wide selection of produce and, because everything's in season and grown locally, it should prove good value for money.

Select own-brand products

Although cost can often indicate quality, this isn't always the case, and cheaper own-brand products are often just as good as the more expensive branded ones. Shop around and decide for yourself what's worth spending more on and when the cheaper option is just as good.

Stocking up your storecupboard

A well-stocked storecupboard is essential for any cook, but when you're looking to put together meals on a budget it's even more important. You don't want to find yourself ready to start cooking only to realize that you're missing an all-important ingredient and have to pop out to the nearest and maybe more expensive shop, thereby costing you extra money and time. And if you keep a good storecupboard you can take advantage of all kinds of offers in the supermarket and economize in that way. Many storecupboard ingredients are fundamentally economical too – pasta, rice and grains are tasty and cheap, and fantastic for filling up hungry families. And ingredients such as canned tuna and sardines can be cheaper than fresh and have the added advantage of a long shelf life, so you're not restricted as to when you have to use them up. Canned vegetables such as tomatoes and sweetcorn are also inexpensive and versatile, and invaluable for cooking up a cheap meal in a matter of minutes.

Choose the basics

Make sure that you've got a wide variety of carbohydrates to serve with your meals, or to make meals with. Noodles, pasta (both long strands and short shapes), rice and couscous all make good choices because they've got a long shelf life and are incredibly versatile. Try them in dishes such as Mixed Bean Kedgeree, page 114, Pasta Pie, page 118, Pasta with Tomato & Basil Sauce, page 110, or Teriyaki Chicken served with egg noodles, page 152. Canned ingredients are essential in every storecupboard and, in addition to the vegetables mentioned above, beans and pulses, canned fruit such as apricots and pineapple, tuna and coconut milk are all indispensable. Other dried essentials include herbs and spices, salt and pepper, and flour

and sugar. Oil (olive and a flavourless oil such as vegetable or sunflower) together with vinegar and other condiments such as mustard, vinegar and soy sauce are also vital storecupboard supplies, central to cooking and flavouring countless dishes from salads and stir-fries to soups and stews.

Check out the bulk buys

Most supermarkets have offers every week for fantastic bulk buys that seem to provide great value for money, but always stop and think before you pile these bargains into your trolley. Will you be able to use up what you're buying? If you can't, then you're wasting food and money, so this cheap deal may not be quite as advantageous as it appears. A giant tin of baked beans isn't a bargain if you can only use up half of it, but three cans of

tomatoes for the price of two that you can keep in the storecupboard might well be worth buying.

Check out the price
Often buying in larger quantities is cheaper, and most supermarkets show not only the pack price but the unit price too, so you can see if what you're buying is a bargain per gram or per kilo. For ingredients such as pasta or rice that you frequently use, it's usually more economical to buy one large packet to keep in the storecupboard rather than two smaller ones.

Check out the shelf life
Some dry ingredients such as dried herbs and ground spices have a relatively short shelf life and lose their flavour after a time, so unless you use them very regularly you might be better off buying them in smaller amounts.

Similarly, nuts and oils can turn rancid over time, so it's important to buy in quantities that you will use before the use-by date is up.

Fantastic freezing
The home freezer can be an absolute boon to the budget cook and can also be a real time-saver. You can buy ready-frozen ingredients from the supermarket to store in your freezer, or you can freeze your own ingredients such as fruit and vegetables at home. Either freeze them as plain ingredients, or cook them up in soups, sauces, casseroles or desserts that freeze well, so you've got ready-prepared, homemade meals available in the freezer.

Because freezer items have a long shelf life, you can buy ingredients in bulk, which can often prove cheaper. You can buy big bags of vegetables or prawns, for example, and just throw a handful into dishes as required. However, foods can't be frozen indefinitely and most should be used up within around three months, so always check the label and don't buy more than you know you can use up. If you freeze your own produce, always label it with the date of freezing.

Choose quality ingredients
Some ingredients such as peas and sweetcorn are often better frozen than fresh. The natural sugars in these vegetables start to turn to starch as soon as they are

of time that will out-shine their ready-made commercial counterparts in taste and undercut them in cost. Fresh stock, for instance, makes for perfect homemade soups and risottos, such as Tomato Risoni Soup, page 32, and Carrot, Pea & Broad Bean Risotto, page 104, while frozen pastry – both puff and shortcrust – can be used to create such delicious delights as Caramelized Banana Puff Tart, page 218, Apricot Tartlets, page 204, and Strawberry & Blueberry Tartlets, page 234.

picked, so unless you can be sure of a really fresh source you'll often get better-quality ingredients by buying the frozen variety because they are processed so soon after harvesting.

Save time and money
Because most ingredients such as fruit, vegetables, meat, poultry and fish are prepared before freezing, it can save you time in the kitchen, and time often means money! Although you might need to remember to allow time for your chicken to thaw out before cooking, transferring some chicken pieces from the freezer to the refrigerator is easier than jointing a whole chicken. It's also worth keeping a supply of quality time-saving ingredients ready in the freezer so that you can make upmarket dishes in the minimum

Seasonal bargains
Frozen ingredients can often prove a better choice when fresh ones are out of season. And when the fresh ingredients are in season why not buy them in bulk when they're cheap and in abundance and freeze them yourself at home? Berries, for example, are easy to freeze, and it means you can enjoy them at summer prices long after summer is over.

Grow your own
If you grow your own fruit and vegetables, you can often end up with gluts of produce, so rather than wasting these valuable ingredients why not freeze them?

Take advantage of offers
Save money with bulk-buy offers and store what you don't need in the freezer for a later date.

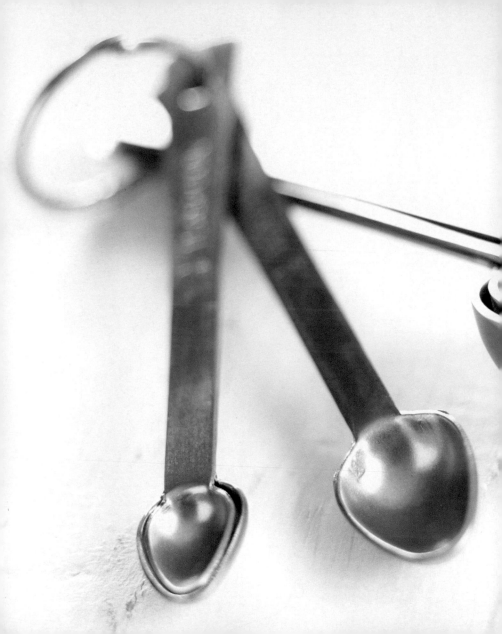

starters & snacks

Camembert 'fondue'

Serves **4**
Preparation time **10 minutes**
Cooking time **5–10 minutes**

1 whole **Camembert cheese**,
   250 g (8 oz) in weight
2 tablespoons **olive oil**
leaves stripped from
   2 **rosemary sprigs**
crusty **French bread**
50 g (2 oz) **walnuts**, roughly
   chopped and toasted
2 tablespoons **clear honey**

Put the Camembert in an ovenproof dish. Make a few cuts in the top, then drizzle with the oil and sprinkle with the rosemary leaves.

Cover with foil and bake in a preheated oven, 200°C (400°F), Gas Mark 6, for 5–10 minutes until gooey.

Cut the French bread into chunky pieces and lightly toast until golden brown.

Sprinkle the walnuts over the cooked Camembert, drizzle with the honey and serve immediately with the toasted chunks of bread.

For Brie & hazelnut 'fondue', use a 250 g (8 oz) round of Brie instead of the Camembert and sprinkle 50 g (2 oz) chopped, toasted hazelnuts over the baked cheese in place of the walnuts.

tomato & mozzarella tartlets

Serves **6**
Preparation time **20 minutes**
Cooking time **20 minutes**

250 g (8 oz) **puff pastry**,
   defrosted if frozen
6 tablespoons **sun-dried
   tomato paste**
3 **plum tomatoes**, deseeded
   and roughly chopped
125 g (4 oz) **mozzarella
   cheese**, roughly diced
8 **pitted black olives**, roughly
   chopped
1 **garlic clove**, finely chopped
2 tablespoons roughly
   chopped **oregano**
1 tablespoon **pine nuts**
olive oil, for drizzling
salt and pepper

Line a large baking sheet with nonstick baking paper. Roll out the pastry on a lightly floured work surface to 2.5 mm (⅛ inch) thick. Use a 12 cm (5 inch) round cutter to stamp out 6 rounds and lay on the prepared baking sheet.

Spread 1 tablespoon sun-dried tomato paste over each pastry round. In a small bowl, mix together the tomatoes, mozzarella, olives, garlic, oregano and pine nuts and season well with salt and pepper. Divide the mixture between the pastry rounds.

Drizzle a little olive oil over the tartlets and bake in a preheated oven, 200°C (400°F), Gas Mark 6, for 20 minutes or until the pastry is golden. Serve immediately with mixed salad leaves.

For tomato & anchovy tartlets, follow the first stage of the recipe, then spread 1 tablespoon pesto over each pastry round instead of the sun-dried tomato paste. In a bowl, mix the tomatoes, olives and garlic, as above, with a 50 g (2 oz) can anchovy fillets in oil, drained and snipped into small pieces, 50 g (2 oz) drained and chopped bottled roasted red peppers in oil and 2 tablespoons chopped basil and season well with salt and pepper. Divide between the pastry rounds, drizzle with olive oil and bake as above.

goats' cheese & chive soufflés

Serves **4**
Preparation time **10 minutes**
Cooking time **20–25 minutes**

25 g (1 oz) **unsalted butter**
2 tablespoons **plain flour**
250 ml (8 fl oz) **milk**
100 g (3½ oz) **soft goats' cheese**
3 **eggs**, separated
2 tablespoons chopped **chives**
salt and pepper

Melt the butter in a saucepan, add the flour and cook over a low heat, stirring, for 30 seconds. Remove the pan from the heat and gradually stir in the milk until smooth. Return to the heat and cook, stirring constantly, until the mixture thickens. Cook for 1 minute.

Leave to cool slightly, then beat in the goats' cheese, egg yolks, chives, and salt and pepper to taste.

Whisk the egg whites in a large, perfectly clean bowl, until soft peaks form. Fold the egg whites into the cheese mixture. Spoon the mixture into 4 greased, individual soufflé ramekins and set on a baking sheet. Bake in a preheated oven, 200°C (400°F), Gas Mark 6, for 15–18 minutes until risen and golden. Serve immediately.

For Cheddar & chilli soufflés, use 100 g (3½ oz) grated Cheddar cheese instead of soft goats' cheese and 2 tablespoons finely chopped coriander leaves in place of the chives, and also beat 2 finely chopped red chillies, deseeded according to taste, into the egg yolk mixture.

potato & bacon cakes

Serves **4**
Preparation time **15 minutes**,
   plus chilling
Cooking time **about
   45 minutes**

1 kg (2 lb) **potatoes**, cut
   into chunks
vegetable oil, for shallow-
   frying
6 **spring onions**, sliced
200 g (7 oz) **back bacon**,
   chopped
2 tablespoons chopped
   flat leaf parsley
plain flour, for coating
25 g (1 oz) **butter**
salt and pepper

For the tomato sauce
200 ml (7 fl oz) **crème fraîche**
2 tablespoons chopped **basil**
2 tablespoons chopped
   tomatoes

Cook the potatoes in a large saucepan of salted
boiling water for 15–20 minutes until tender. Drain
well, return to the pan and mash.

Heat a little oil in a frying pan, add the spring onions
and cook for 2–3 minutes, then add the bacon and
cook until browned. Add to the mash with the parsley.
Season well with salt and pepper. Form the potato
mixture into 8 cakes, then cover and chill in the
refrigerator until firm.

Lightly coat the cakes in flour. Melt the butter in a
nonstick frying pan, add the cakes, in batches, and
cook over a medium heat for 4–5 minutes on each
side until browned and heated through.

Meanwhile, to make the sauce, put the crème fraîche
in a bowl and mix in the basil and tomatoes. Season
well with salt and pepper.

Serve the cakes hot with the sauce.

**For salmon fishcakes with soured cream &
mushroom sauce**, use a 200 g (7 oz) can red
salmon instead of the bacon. Drain and flake the
salmon into the mashed potato mixture. Form into
cakes and cook as above. Meanwhile, melt 25 g
(1 oz) butter in a saucepan, add 100 g (3½ oz)
sliced button mushrooms and cook for 1 minute.
Stir in 200 ml (7 fl oz) soured cream and ¼ teaspoon
paprika and season to taste with salt and pepper.
Heat through gently and serve with the fishcakes.

aubergine, tomato & feta rolls

Serves **4**
Preparation time **15 minutes**
Cooking time **about**
  6 minutes

2 **aubergines**
3 tablespoons **olive oil**
125 g (4 oz) **feta cheese**,
  roughly diced
12 **sun-dried tomatoes in oil**,
  drained
15–20 **basil leaves**
salt and pepper

Trim the ends of the aubergines, then cut a thin slice lengthways from either side of each; discard these slices, which should be mainly skin. Cut each aubergine lengthways into 4 slices. Heat the grill on the hottest setting or heat a griddle pan until very hot.

Brush both sides of the aubergine slices with the oil, then cook under the grill or in the griddle pan for 3 minutes on each side or until browned and softened.

Lay the aubergine slices on a board and divide the feta, tomatoes and basil leaves between them. Season well with salt and pepper. Roll up each slice from a short end and secure with a cocktail stick. Arrange on serving plates and serve immediately, or cover and set aside in a cool place, but not the refrigerator, and serve at room temperature when required.

For courgette & mozzarella rolls, use 3–4 large courgettes, then trim the ends and sides as for the aubergines. Cut each courgette lengthways into 3 slices, depending on their thickness, brush with oil and cook under the grill or in a griddle pan as for the aubergines until browned and softened. Spread the courgette slices with red pesto, then top with 125 g (4 oz) diced mozzarella cheese and the basil leaves. Roll up and serve as above.

mixed bean salsa with tortilla chips

Serves **4**
Preparation time **10 minutes**,
  plus standing

2 x 400 g (13 oz) cans **mixed
  beans**, drained and rinsed
3 **tomatoes**, chopped
1 **red pepper**, cored,
  deseeded and finely diced
6 **spring onions**, sliced
1 teaspoon finely chopped
  red chilli
2 tablespoons **olive oil**
1 tablespoon **white wine
  vinegar**
chopped **coriander**, to garnish
salt and pepper

To serve
tortilla chips
soured cream

Put the beans, tomatoes, red pepper and spring onions in a food processor and blend until fairly smooth.

In a small bowl, whisk together the chilli, oil and vinegar, pour over the bean mixture and toss to coat. Season to taste with salt and pepper and garnish with coriander. Cover and leave to stand at room temperature for about 30 minutes to allow the flavours to mingle.

Serve the salsa with tortilla chips and soured cream.

For mixed bean pilau, which will work as a substantial starter or side dish, add 375 g (12 oz) basmati rice to a pan, cover with 600 ml (1 pint) water and bring to the boil. Reduce the heat, cover and simmer for 12 minutes without removing the lid. Remove from the heat, toss in the mixed bean salsa (see above) and stir in 3 tablespoons chopped coriander leaves. Replace the lid and return to a very low heat for 5 minutes. Serve hot.

onion & mushroom quesadillas

Serves **4**
Preparation time **10 minutes**
Cooking time **about
  30 minutes**

3 tablespoons **olive oil**
2 **red onions**, thinly sliced
1 teaspoon **caster sugar**
8 **flour tortillas**
200 g (7 oz) **button
  mushrooms**, sliced
150 g (5 oz) **Cheddar
  cheese**, grated
a small handful of **parsley**,
  chopped
salt and pepper

Heat 2 tablespoons of the oil in a large frying pan, add the onions and cook until soft. Add the sugar and cook for 3 minutes or until caramelized. Remove the onions with a slotted spoon and set aside. Heat the remaining oil in the pan, add the mushrooms and cook for 3 minutes or until golden brown. Set aside.

Heat a nonstick frying pan and add 1 tortilla. Scatter over a quarter of the red onions, mushrooms, Cheddar and parsley. Season to taste with salt and pepper. Cover with another tortilla and cook until browned on the underside. Turn over and cook until browned on the other side. Remove from the pan and keep warm.

Repeat with the remaining tortillas and ingredients. Cut into wedges and serve with a salad.

For spinach & Brie quesadillas, replace the mushrooms with 200 g (7 oz) cooked, chopped spinach leaves and use 150 g (5 oz) Brie, cut into slices, instead of the Cheddar. Cook and serve as above.

fried goats' cheese

Serves **4**
Preparation time **15 minutes**
Cooking time **10 minutes**

4 individual **goats' cheeses**,
    about 65 g (2½ oz) each
2 **eggs**, beaten
4 tablespoons **fresh white
    breadcrumbs**
about 200 ml (7 fl oz)
    vegetable oil, for
    deep-frying
125 g (4 oz) **rocket leaves**
2 tablespoons **olive oil**
salt and pepper

For red onion marmalade
1 tablespoon **olive oil**
2 **red onions**, thinly sliced
125 ml (4 fl oz) **red wine**
3 tablespoons **red wine
    vinegar**
50 g (2 oz) **caster sugar**

Dip the cheeses in the beaten egg and then coat evenly with the breadcrumbs. Cover and chill while you prepare the onion marmalade.

Heat the olive oil in a small saucepan, add the onions and cook for 2 minutes. Stir in the wine, vinegar and sugar, then cook for 5 minutes or until the onions are translucent. Remove with a slotted spoon and set aside, reserving the juices in the pan.

Heat the vegetable oil in a nonstick frying pan to 180–190°C (350–375°F) or until a cube of bread browns in 30 seconds. (Take care not to overfill the frying pan. If necessary, use a saucepan or deep frying pan.) Add the goats' cheeses and cook for 2 minutes or until golden. Remove with a slotted spoon and drain well on kitchen paper.

Divide the rocket between 4 plates and drizzle the olive oil and reserved juices from the onions over the top. Season to taste with salt and pepper. Place the goats' cheeses on the rocket and top with the onion marmalade. Serve immediately.

For fried Camembert & tomato-chilli sauce, cut a 250 g (8 oz) Camembert into wedges, coat and chill as above. Bring a 400 g (13 oz) can chopped tomatoes, 2–3 finely chopped red chillies, 2 crushed garlic cloves, 125 g (4 oz) soft light brown sugar, 4 tablespoons white wine vinegar, 1 tablespoon Worcestershire sauce and ½ teaspoon salt to the boil in a saucepan. Reduce the heat and simmer gently for 30 minutes or until thick. Cook the Camembert as above and serve with the sauce.

tomato risoni soup

Serves **4**
Preparation time **10 minutes**
Cooking time **18 minutes**

2 tablespoons **olive oil**, plus
  extra for drizzling
1 large **onion**, finely chopped
2 **celery sticks**, finely
  chopped
4 **large tomatoes**
1.5 litres (2½ pints) **vegetable
  stock**
150 g (5 oz) **dried risoni or
  orzo** or any tiny shaped
  dried pasta
6 tablespoons finely chopped
  flat leaf parsley
salt and pepper

Heat the oil in a large saucepan over a medium heat, add the onion and celery and cook until soft.

Meanwhile, score a cross in the base of each tomato, then put in a heatproof bowl of boiling water for 1 minute. Plunge into cold water, then peel the skin away from the cross. Halve the tomatoes, then scoop out the seeds and discard. Roughly chop the flesh.

Add the tomatoes, stock, onions and celery to the pan and bring to the boil. Add the pasta and cook for 10 minutes or until al dente. Season to taste with salt and pepper and stir in the parsley.

Remove from the heat, ladle into warmed bowls and drizzle with oil before serving.

For homemade vegetable stock, put 625 g (1¼ lb) mixed vegetables (excluding potatoes, parsnips and other starchy root vegetables), 2 peeled garlic cloves, 8 peppercorns and 1 bouquet garni in a large saucepan, add 1.8 litres (3 pints) water and bring to the boil. Reduce the heat and simmer gently for 40 minutes, skimming any scum that rises to the surface. Strain through a muslin-lined sieve. If not using straight away, leave to cool before covering and refrigerating.

sweetcorn & pepper frittata

Serves **4**
Preparation time **10 minutes**
Cooking time **about**
  10 minutes

2 tablespoons **olive oil**
4 **spring onions**, thinly sliced
200 g (7 oz) can **sweetcorn**,
  drained
150 g (5 oz) bottled **roasted
  red peppers** in oil, drained
  and cut into strips
4 **eggs**, lightly beaten
125 g (4 oz) **strong Cheddar
  cheese**, grated
1 small handful of **chives**,
  finely chopped
salt and pepper

Heat the oil in a frying pan, add the spring onions,
sweetcorn and red peppers and cook for 30 seconds.

Add the eggs, Cheddar, chives, and salt and pepper to
taste and cook over a medium heat for 4–5 minutes
until the base is set. Remove from the hob, place under
a preheated grill and cook for 3–4 minutes or until
golden and set. Cut into wedges and serve immediately
with a green salad and crusty bread.

For courgette, pepper & Gruyère frittata, use
200 g (7 oz) finely chopped courgettes instead of the
sweetcorn, 125 g (4 oz) grated Gruyère cheese in
place of the Cheddar and substitute 4 tablespoons
chopped mint leaves for the chives.

risi e bisi

Serves **4**
Preparation time **5 minutes**
Cooking time **about
   25 minutes**

1 tablespoon **butter**
1 tablespoon **olive oil**
1 **onion**, finely chopped
2 **garlic cloves**, crushed
250 g (8 oz) **risotto rice**
900 ml (1½ pints) **hot chicken
   stock**, made with 1 chicken
   stock cube and boiling
   water, heated to simmering
450 g (14½ oz) **frozen peas**
25 g (1 oz) **Parmesan
   cheese**, grated
100 g (3½ oz) **cooked ham**,
   finely chopped
1 bunch of **parsley**, finely
   chopped
salt and pepper

Melt the butter with the oil in a saucepan, add the onion and garlic and cook until the onion is soft and starting to brown. Add the rice and stir until coated with the butter mixture.

Add the hot stock, a ladleful at a time, and cook, stirring constantly, until each addition has been absorbed before adding the next. Continue until all the stock has been absorbed and the rice is creamy and cooked but still retains a little bite – this will take around 15 minutes.

Add the peas and heat through for 3–5 minutes. Remove from the heat and stir in the Parmesan, ham and parsley. Season to taste with salt and pepper and serve immediately.

For tuna & tomato risotto, after cooking the onion and garlic, add 3 tablespoons white wine and cook, stirring, until it has evaporated. Then follow the recipe above, but use fish stock instead of chicken stock and add 2 chopped tomatoes in place of the peas, along with a 200 g (7 oz) can tuna, drained and flaked, and heat through for 3–5 minutes. Remove from the heat and stir in 2 tablespoons chopped basil leaves with the Parmesan cheese and salt and pepper to taste. Serve immediately.

minted pea soup

Serves **4**
Preparation time **10 minutes**
Cooking time **20 minutes**

1 tablespoon **butter**
1 **onion**, finely chopped
1 **potato**, finely chopped
1 litre (1¾ pints) **vegetable stock**
400 g (13 oz) **frozen peas**
6 tablespoons finely chopped **mint leaves**
salt and pepper
crème fraîche (optional), to serve

Melt the butter in a saucepan, add the onion and potato and cook for 5 minutes. Add the stock and bring to the boil, then reduce heat and simmer gently for 10 minutes or until the potato is tender.

Add the peas to the pan and cook for a further 3–4 minutes. Season well with salt and pepper, remove from the heat and stir in the mint. Purée in a food processor or blender until smooth. Ladle into warmed bowls and top each with a dollop of crème fraîche, if liked.

For chunky pea & ham soup, cook 1 chopped carrot and 1 chopped turnip with the onion and potato, then add 1 litre (1¾ pints) ham or chicken stock. Once the root vegetables are tender, add 300 g (10 oz) chopped cooked ham, 4 finely chopped spring onions and 2 tablespoons chopped parsley with the peas and cook for 3–4 minutes. Do not blend the soup, but ladle into warmed bowls and serve with crusty bread.

goats' cheese & tomato tarts

Serves **4**
Preparation time **15 minutes**
Cooking time **10–12 minutes**

4 sheets of **filo pastry**, about
    25 cm (10 inches) square
    each
1 tablespoon **olive oil**
20 **cherry tomatoes**, halved
200 g (7 oz) **firm goats'
    cheese**, cut into 1 cm
    (½ inch) cubes
20 g (¾ oz) **pine nuts**
2 teaspoons **thyme leaves**
salt and pepper

Lightly oil 4 individual tartlet tins, each about 10 cm
(4 inches) in diameter. Brush a sheet of filo pastry
with a little of the oil. Cut in half, then across into
4 equal-sized squares and use to line one of the tins.
Repeat with the remaining pastry sheets. Brush any
remaining oil over the pastry in the tins.

Put 5 tomato halves in the bottom of each tartlet. Top
with the goats' cheese, then add the remaining tomato
halves and pine nuts. Sprinkle with the thyme leaves
and season well with salt and pepper.

Bake the tartlets in a preheated oven, 200°C (400°F),
Gas Mark 6, for 10–12 minutes or until the pastry is
crisp and golden. Serve hot with a leafy green salad.

For feta & pepper tarts, roll out 175 g (6 oz)
puff pastry on a lightly floured work surface and use
to line the tartlet tins. Core and deseed 1 yellow and
1 orange pepper, then slice into thin strips and toss
in a little olive oil. Cut 200 g (7 oz) feta cheese into
1 cm (½ inch) cubes. Divide half the pepper strips
between the tartlets, top with the cheese, then add
the remaining pepper strips, and scatter over the pine
nuts, as above. Sprinkle with 2 teaspoons dried
oregano and season well with salt and pepper. Bake
at the same temperature as specified above for about
15 minutes or until the pastry is golden.

vegetable &
salad dishes

spinach & potato gratin

Serves **4**
Preparation time **10 minutes**
Cooking time **35 minutes**

625 g (1¼ lb) **potatoes**,
   thinly sliced
500 g (1 lb) **spinach leaves**
200 g (7 oz) **mozzarella
   cheese**, grated
4 **tomatoes**, sliced
3 **eggs**, beaten
300 ml (½ pint) **whipping
   cream**
salt and pepper

Cook the potato slices in a large saucepan of salted boiling water for 5 minutes, then drain well.

Meanwhile, cook the spinach in a separate saucepan of boiling water for 1–2 minutes. Drain and squeeze out the excess water.

Grease a large ovenproof dish and line the bottom with half the potato slices. Cover with the spinach and half the mozzarella, seasoning each layer well with salt and pepper. Cover with the remaining potato slices and arrange the tomato slices on top. Sprinkle with the remaining mozzarella.

Whisk the eggs and cream together in a bowl and season well with salt and pepper. Pour over the ingredients in the dish.

Bake in a preheated oven, 180°C (350°F), Gas Mark 4, for about 30 minutes. Serve immediately with a salad and crusty bread.

For tomato, lime & basil salad to serve as an accompaniment, slice or quarter 1 kg (2 lb) tomatoes while the gratin is baking, and arrange in a large serving bowl. Scatter over ½ red onion, thinly sliced, and 1 handful of basil leaves. Whisk together 4 tablespoons olive oil, 2 tablespoons chopped basil, 1 tablespoon lime juice, 1 teaspoon grated lime rind, ½ teaspoon clear honey, 1 crushed garlic clove, a pinch of cayenne pepper, and salt and pepper to taste. Pour over the salad. Cover and leave to stand at room temperature for about 30 minutes to allow the flavours to mingle, then serve with the gratin.

mushroom stroganoff

Serves **4**
Preparation time **10 minutes**
Cooking time **10 minutes**

1 tablespoon **butter**
2 tablespoons **olive oil**
1 **onion**, thinly sliced
4 **garlic cloves**, finely
   chopped
500 g (1 lb) **chestnut
   mushrooms**, sliced
2 tablespoons **wholegrain
   mustard**
250 ml (8 fl oz) **crème fraîche**
salt and pepper
3 tablespoons chopped
   parsley, to garnish

Melt the butter with the oil in a large frying pan, add
the onion and garlic and cook until soft and starting
to brown.

Add the mushrooms to the pan and cook until soft and
starting to brown. Stir in the mustard and crème fraîche
and just heat through. Season to taste with salt and
pepper, then serve immediately, garnished with the
chopped parsley.

For mushroom soup with garlic croûtons, while
the mushrooms are cooking, remove the crusts
from 2 thick slices of day-old white bread and rub
with 2 halved garlic cloves. Cut the bread into cubes.
Fry the cubes of bread in a shallow depth of
vegetable oil in a frying pan, turning constantly, for
5 minutes or until browned all over and crisp. Drain
on kitchen paper. After adding the mustard and
crème fraîche to the mushroom mixture as above, add
400 ml (14 fl oz) boiling hot vegetable stock, then
purée the mixture in a food processor or blender until
smooth. Serve in warmed bowls, topped with the
croûtons and garnished with the chopped parsley.

greek vegetable casserole

Serves **4**

Preparation time **10 minutes**

Cooking time **25 minutes**

4 tablespoons **olive oil**

1 **onion**, thinly sliced

3 **peppers** of mixed colours,
   cored, deseeded and sliced
   into rings

4 **garlic cloves**, crushed

4 **tomatoes**, chopped

200 g (7 oz) **feta cheese**,
   cubed

1 teaspoon **dried oregano**

salt and pepper

chopped **flat leaf parsley**,
   to garnish

Heat 3 tablespoons of the oil in a flameproof casserole, add the onion, peppers and garlic and cook until soft and starting to brown. Add the tomatoes and cook for a few minutes until softened. Mix in the feta and oregano, season to taste with salt and pepper and drizzle with the remaining oil.

Cover and cook in a preheated oven, 200°C (400°F), Gas Mark 6, for 15 minutes. Garnish with the parsley and serve with warmed crusty bread.

For Middle Eastern vegetable casserole, heat 1 tablespoon olive oil in a flameproof casserole, add 1 red onion, cut into wedges, 3 sliced celery sticks and 3 thinly sliced carrots and cook until soft and starting to brown. Add 2 teaspoons harissa and cook, stirring, for 1 minute. Add about 625 g (1¼ lb) aubergines, trimmed and chopped, 2 large chopped tomatoes and 250 ml (8 fl oz) water. Bring to the boil, then cover and cook in a preheated oven, 180°C (350°F), Gas Mark 4, for about 25 minutes. Stir in 2 large potatoes, peeled and thickly sliced, and cook for a further 15 minutes or until tender but still firm. Serve hot garnished with chopped coriander.

golden mushroom & leek pies

Serves **4**
Preparation time **15 minutes**
Cooking time **25–30 minutes**

25 g (1 oz) **butter**
2 **leeks**, thinly sliced
300 g (10 oz) **chestnut mushrooms**, quartered
300 g (10 oz) **button mushrooms**, quartered
1 tablespoon **plain flour**
250 ml (8 fl oz) **milk**
150 ml (¼ pint) **double cream**
100 g (3½ oz) **strong Cheddar cheese**, grated
4 tablespoons finely chopped **parsley**
2 sheets of **ready-rolled puff pastry**, defrosted if frozen
1 **egg**, beaten

Melt the butter in a large saucepan, add the leeks and cook for 1–2 minutes. Add the mushrooms and cook for 2 minutes. Stir in the flour and cook, stirring, for 1 minute, then gradually add the milk and cream and cook, stirring constantly, until the mixture thickens. Add the Cheddar and the parsley and cook, stirring, for 1–2 minutes. Remove from the heat.

Cut 4 rounds from the pastry sheets to cover 4 individual pie dishes. Divide the mushroom mixture between the pie dishes. Brush the rims with the beaten egg, then place the pastry rounds on top. Press down around the rims and crimp the edges with a fork. Cut a couple of slits in the top of each pie to let the steam out. Brush the pastry with the remaining egg.

Bake in a preheated oven, 220°C (425°F), Gas Mark 7, for 15–20 minutes until the pastry is golden brown. Serve immediately.

For curried ham & mushroom pies, follow the first stage above, but after cooking the mushrooms add 1 teaspoon medium curry powder and ½ teaspoon turmeric to the pan and cook, stirring, for 1 minute, before adding the flour and continuing with the recipe. Once the sauce has thickened, stir in 200 g (7 oz) cooked ham, cut into small bite-sized pieces, in place of the Cheddar and 4 tablespoons chopped coriander leaves instead of the parsley. Make and bake the pies as above.

grilled chicory with salsa verde

Serves **4**
Preparation time **15 minutes**
Cooking time **10 minutes**

4 **heads of chicory**, about
    150 g (5 oz) each, trimmed
    and halved lengthways
2 tablespoons **olive oil**
125 g (4 oz) **Parmesan**
    cheese, coarsely grated
chopped **parsley**, to garnish

For the salsa verde
200 g (7 oz) **flat leaf parsley**
50 g (2 oz) **pine nuts**, toasted
2 **pickled gherkins**
8 **pitted green olives**
1 **garlic clove**, chopped
1 tablespoon **lemon juice**
150 ml (¼ pint) **olive oil**
salt and pepper

Coarsely purée all the ingredients for the salsa verde, except the oil, in a food processor or blender. With the motor still running, gradually trickle in the oil to make a creamy paste. Transfer to a serving dish, cover and set aside. (The salsa will keep for up to 1 week in the refrigerator.)

Heat the grill on the hottest setting. Arrange the chicory halves on the grill rack, cut-sides down, brush with some of the oil and cook under the grill for 5 minutes. Turn the chicory halves over, brush with the remaining oil and sprinkle the Parmesan over the top. Cook for a further 4 minutes or until the cheese has melted and the edges of the chicory begin to char.

Transfer the chicory to plates and garnish with chopped parsley. Add a little salsa verde to each plate and serve immediately, offering the remaining salsa verde separately. Toasted ciabatta bread is a good accompaniment.

For grilled sardines with salsa verde, arrange 750 g (1½ lb) whole, cleaned and gutted sardines in a large, shallow, glass or ceramic dish. Whisk together 3 tablespoons olive oil, 2 garlic cloves, the grated rind and juice of 1 lemon and 2 teaspoons dried oregano. Pour over the fish and turn them in the marinade to coat, then cover and leave to marinate in the refrigerator for about 1 hour. Meanwhile, prepare the salsa verde as above. Cook the sardines under a preheated grill or over a barbecue for 4–5 minutes on each side, basting with the marinade. Serve with the salsa verde.

curried cauliflower with chickpeas

Serves **4**

Preparation time **10 minutes**

Cooking time **20 minutes**

2 tablespoons **olive oil**

1 **onion**, chopped

2 **garlic cloves**, crushed

4 tablespoons **medium curry paste**

1 **small cauliflower**, divided into florets

375 ml (13 fl oz) **vegetable stock**, made with 1 vegetable stock cube and boiling water

4 **tomatoes**, roughly chopped

400 g (13 oz) canned **chickpeas**, drained and rinsed

2 tablespoons **mango chutney**

salt and pepper

4 tablespoons chopped **coriander**, to garnish

whisked **natural yogurt**, to serve (optional)

Heat the oil in a saucepan, add the onion and garlic and cook until the onion is soft and starting to brown. Stir in the curry paste, add the cauliflower and stock and bring to the boil. Reduce the heat, cover tightly and simmer for 10 minutes.

Add the tomatoes, chickpeas and chutney and continue to cook, uncovered, for 10 minutes. Season to taste with salt and pepper. Serve garnished with coriander and drizzled with a little whisked yogurt, if liked.

For homemade mango chutney, put the peeled, stoned and sliced flesh of 6 ripe mangoes in a large saucepan with 300 ml (½ pint) white wine vinegar and cook over a low heat for 10 minutes. Add 250 g (8 oz) soft dark brown sugar, 50 g (2 oz) fresh root ginger, peeled and finely chopped, 2 crushed garlic cloves, 2 teaspoons chilli powder and 1 teaspoon salt and bring to the boil, stirring constantly. Reduce the heat and simmer for 30 minutes, stirring occasionally. Ladle into a sterilized screw-top jar and replace the lid. Store in the refrigerator and use within 1 month.

quick one-pot ratatouille

Serves **4**

Preparation time **10 minutes**

Cooking time **20 minutes**

100 ml (3½ fl oz) **olive oil**

2 **onions**, chopped

1 medium **aubergine**, cut into bite-sized cubes

2 **large courgettes**, cut into bite-sized pieces

1 **red pepper**, cored, deseeded and cut into bite-sized pieces

1 **yellow pepper**, cored, deseeded and cut into bite-sized pieces

2 **garlic cloves**, crushed

400 g (13 oz) can **chopped tomatoes**

4 tablespoons chopped **parsley** or **basil**

salt and pepper

Heat the oil in a large saucepan until very hot, add the onions, aubergine, courgettes, peppers and garlic and cook, stirring constantly, for a few minutes until softened. Add the tomatoes, season to taste with salt and pepper and stir well.

Reduce the heat, cover the pan tightly and simmer for 15 minutes until all the vegetables are cooked. Remove from the heat and stir in the chopped parsley or basil before serving.

For Mediterranean vegetable pie, spoon the cooked vegetable mixture into a medium-sized ovenproof dish. Cook 800 g (1 lb 10 oz) quartered potatoes in a large saucepan of salted boiling water for 12–15 minutes or until tender, then drain and roughly mash with 200 g (7 oz) finely grated Cheddar cheese. Spread over the vegetable mixture, then bake in a preheated oven, 180°C (350°F), Gas Mark 4, for 20 minutes or until lightly golden on top.

baked aubergines & mozzarella

Serves **4**

Preparation time **10 minutes**

Cooking time **about**
  25 minutes

2 **aubergines**, sliced in
  half lengthways
3 tablespoons **olive oil**
1 **onion**, chopped
1 **garlic clove**, crushed
250 g (8 oz) can **chopped**
  tomatoes
1 tablespoon **tomato purée**
300 g (10 oz) **mozzarella**
  cheese, cut into thin slices
salt and pepper
basil, to garnish

Brush the aubergines with 2 tablespoons of the oil
and arrange, cut-side up, on a baking sheet. Roast
in a preheated oven, 200°C (400°F), Gas Mark 6, for
20 minutes.

Meanwhile, heat the remaining oil in a frying pan, add
the onion and garlic and cook until the onion is soft
and starting to brown. Add the tomatoes and tomato
purée and simmer for 5 minutes or until the sauce
has thickened.

Remove the aubergines from the oven and cover
each half with some sauce and 2 of the mozzarella
slices. Season to taste with salt and pepper and return
to the oven for 4–5 minutes to melt the cheese. Serve
immediately scattered with basil leaves.

For roasted garlic bread to serve as an
accompaniment, separate 2 garlic bulbs into separate
cloves. Put on a square of foil and drizzle generously
with olive oil. Bring up the sides of the foil and twist
together at the top. Bake in the oven alongside the
aubergines, then unwrap and allow to cool slightly
before squeezing the flesh from the skins and
spreading on to slices of hot French bread. Serve
with the baked aubergines.

lebanese lentil & bulgar salad

Serves **4**
Preparation time **10 minutes**
Cooking time **30 minutes**

100 g (3½ oz) **Puy lentils**
1 tablespoon **tomato purée**
750 ml (1¼ pints) **vegetable
  stock**
100 g (3½ oz) **bulgar wheat**
juice of 1 **lemon**
1 tablespoon **olive oil**
2 **onions**, sliced
1 teaspoon **granulated sugar**
1 bunch of **mint**, chopped
salt and pepper
3 **tomatoes**, finely chopped

Put the lentils, tomato purée and stock in a
saucepan and bring to the boil. Reduce the heat,
cover tightly and simmer for 20 minutes. Add the
bulgar wheat and lemon juice and season to taste with
salt and pepper. Cook for 10 minutes until all the stock
has been absorbed.

Meanwhile, heat the oil in a frying pan, add the onions
and sugar and cook over a low heat until deep brown
and caramelized.

Stir the mint into the lentil and bulgar wheat mixture,
then serve warm, topped with the fried onions and
chopped tomato.

For Lebanese-style chicken salad, season
3 chicken breasts with salt and pepper. Brush each
one with a little olive oil and place on a very hot
griddle pan. Cook for 4–5 minutes on each side or
until cooked through and lightly charred on the
edges. Cut the breasts into thin slices and stir into
the lentil salad above with 1 finely chopped cucumber
and 10–12 sliced radishes.

creamy courgettes with walnuts

Serves **4**
Preparation time **10 minutes**
Cooking time **10–15 minutes**

3 tablespoons **olive oil**
1 **onion**, chopped
4 **courgettes**, cut into
  matchsticks
2 **celery sticks**, cut into
  matchsticks
250 g (8 oz) **soft cheese
  with garlic**
100 g (3½ oz) **walnut pieces**
salt and pepper

Heat the oil in a large frying pan, add the onion and cook for 5 minutes until soft. Add the courgettes and celery and cook for 4–5 minutes until soft and starting to brown.

Add the cheese and cook for 2–3 minutes until melted. Stir in the walnuts, season to taste with salt and pepper and serve immediately.

For curried courgettes, cook the onion as above, then add 2 small, quartered potatoes and cook for 2–3 minutes. Stir in the courgettes, sliced, with ½ teaspoon chilli powder, ½ teaspoon turmeric, 1 teaspoon ground coriander and ½ teaspoon salt. Add 150 ml (¼ pint) water, cover and cook over a low heat for 8–10 minutes until the potatoes are tender.

aubergine & courgette salad

Serves **4**
Preparation time **15 minutes**
Cooking time **4–6 minutes**

2 **aubergines**, thinly sliced
2 **courgettes**, thinly sliced
3 tablespoons **olive oil**
125 g (4 oz) **feta cheese**

For the honey-mint dressing
50 g (2 oz) **mint leaves**,
   roughly chopped, plus extra
   leaves to garnish
1 tablespoon **clear honey**
1 teaspoon prepared **English
   mustard**
2 tablespoons **lime juice**
salt and pepper

Brush the aubergine and courgette slices with the oil. Heat the grill on the hottest setting. Cook the vegetables under the grill for 2–3 minutes on each side until lightly cooked.

Arrange the grilled vegetables in a shallow dish. Crumble the feta and sprinkle it over the vegetables.

Whisk all the dressing ingredients together in a small bowl, seasoning to taste with salt and pepper. Pour the dressing over the salad and toss to coat. Scatter with mint leaves to garnish and serve with toasted flat breads or crusty baguette.

For tahini dressing, as an alternative to the honey-mint dressing, put 2 tablespoons tahini paste in a bowl. Slowly beat in 4 tablespoons natural yogurt and 1–2 tablespoons cold water as necessary to make a drizzling consistency. Stir in 2 tablespoons chopped parsley and 1 crushed garlic clove. Season to taste with salt and pepper. Pour over the salad and toss to coat.

thai chicken noodle salad

Serves **4**
Preparation time **10 minutes**
Cooking time **10 minutes**

250 g (8 oz) **thin rice noodles**
6 tablespoons **Thai sweet chilli sauce**
2 tablespoons **Thai fish sauce**
juice of 2 **limes**
2 **cooked boneless, skinless chicken breasts**
1 **cucumber**, cut into ribbons
1 **red chilli**, finely chopped
1 small handful of **coriander leaves**

Put the noodles in a large heatproof bowl and pour boiling water over to cover. Leave for 6–8 minutes until tender, then drain and rinse well under cold running water.

Whisk together the sweet chilli sauce, fish sauce and lime juice in a bowl. Shred the chicken and toss with the dressing to coat.

Add the noodles, cucumber and chilli to the chicken mixture and toss gently to combine. Scatter over the coriander leaves and serve immediately.

For seafood noodle salad, replace the chicken with 500 g (1 lb) cooked peeled prawns and 200 g (7 oz) cooked shelled mussels, and scatter over a small handful of basil leaves instead of coriander leaves.

strawberry & cucumber salad

Serves **4–6**
Preparation time **10 minutes**,
  plus chilling

1 large **cucumber**, halved
  lengthways, deseeded and
  thinly sliced
250 g (8 oz) **strawberries**,
  halved or quartered if large

For the balsamic dressing
1 tablespoon **balsamic
  vinegar**
1 teaspoon **wholegrain
  mustard**
1 teaspoon **clear honey**
3 tablespoons **olive oil**
salt and pepper

Put the cucumber slices and strawberry halves or quarters in a shallow bowl.

Put all the dressing ingredients in a screw-top jar, season to taste with salt and pepper, and shake well.

Pour the dressing over the cucumber and strawberries. Toss gently, then cover and chill for 5–10 minutes before serving.

For cucumber & dill salad, prepare the cucumber as specified above, then put the slices in a colander set over a plate or in the sink. Sprinkle with 2 teaspoons salt and leave to stand for 20–30 minutes, to allow the excess moisture to drain away. Rinse under cold running water, then drain thoroughly and transfer to a shallow serving dish. In a bowl, mix together 4 tablespoons thick Greek yogurt, 1 teaspoon white wine vinegar and 2 tablespoons chopped dill. Season well with pepper. Pour over the cucumber, toss gently to combine and serve garnished with dill sprigs.

76

chickpea & chilli salad

Serves **4**
Preparation time **10 minutes**,
   plus standing

2 x 400 g (13 oz) cans
   chickpeas, drained
   and rinsed
2 **plum tomatoes**, roughly
   chopped
4 **spring onions**, thinly sliced
1 **red chilli**, deseeded and
   thinly sliced
4 tablespoons roughly
   chopped **coriander leaves**
grilled pitta bread, cut into
   thin fingers, to serve

For the lemon dressing
2 tablespoons **lemon juice**
1 **garlic clove**, crushed
2 tablespoons **olive oil**
salt and pepper

Combine all the salad ingredients in a shallow bowl.

Put all the dressing ingredients in a screw-top jar,
season to taste with salt and pepper, and shake
well. Pour over the salad and toss well to coat all
the ingredients.

Cover the salad and leave to stand at room
temperature for about 10 minutes to allow the flavours
to mingle. Serve with grilled pitta bread fingers.

For white bean & sun-dried tomato salad, combine
2 x 400 g (13 oz) cans cannellini beans, drained
and rinsed, 125 g (4 oz) sun-dried tomatoes in oil,
drained and roughly chopped, 1 tablespoon chopped
and pitted black olives, 2 teaspoons drained and
rinsed capers and 2 teaspoons chopped thyme
leaves. Toss in the lemon dressing and leave to
stand as above, then serve with toasted slices of
ciabatta bread.

chorizo, egg & ciabatta salad

Serves **4**
Preparation time **10 minutes**
Cooking time **10 minutes**

½ **ciabatta loaf**, cut into
  chunks
6 tablespoons **olive oil**
2 tablespoons **red wine
  vinegar**
2 teaspoons **wholegrain
  mustard**
4 **eggs**
200 g (7 oz) **chorizo**, thickly
  sliced
4 handfuls of **young spinach
  leaves**
salt and pepper

Toss the ciabatta chunks in 2 tablespoons of the oil, spread out on a baking sheet and bake in a preheated oven, 200°C (400°F), Gas Mark 6, for 10 minutes or until golden brown.

Meanwhile, in a small bowl, whisk together the remaining oil, the vinegar and wholegrain mustard to make the dressing.

Poach the eggs in a large saucepan of barely simmering water for 5 minutes. Fry the chorizo in a dry frying pan over a medium heat for 3–4 minutes or until crisp and cooked through.

Toss the spinach and chorizo in a bowl with a little of the dressing. Divide between 4 plates, scatter over the ciabatta croûtons and top each salad with a poached egg. Drizzle with the remaining dressing, season to taste with salt and pepper and serve immediately.

For fatoush pitta salad, another classic salad that features pieces of bread, in this case pitta bread, combine 2 cored, deseeded and diced green peppers, ½ diced cucumber, 4 diced ripe tomatoes, 1 finely chopped red onion, 2 crushed garlic cloves, 2 tablespoons chopped parsley and 1 tablespoon each of chopped mint and coriander in a large bowl. Toss with the Lemon Dressing on page 78. Toast 2 pitta breads in a preheated griddle pan or under a preheated grill, then tear into bite-sized pieces and stir into the salad. Cover and leave to stand at room temperature for about 30 minutes to allow the flavours to mingle.

greek-style feta salad

Serves **4**
Preparation time **15 minutes**

4 **tomatoes**, cut into wedges
½ **cucumber**, cut into bite-
   sized cubes
1 **green pepper**, cored,
   deseeded and cut into rings
   or thinly sliced
1 **red onion**, thinly sliced
200 g (7 oz) **feta cheese**,
   cubed
100 g (3½ oz) **pitted black
   olives**
4 tablespoons **olive oil**
2 tablespoons **white wine
   vinegar**
2–3 teaspoons finely chopped
   oregano
salt and pepper

Arrange the tomatoes, cucumber, green pepper and
red onion in a serving dish.

Top the salad ingredients with the feta and olives.
Season well with salt and pepper and drizzle with the
oil and vinegar. Serve sprinkled with the oregano.

For watermelon, feta & sunflower seed salad,
add 200 g (7 oz) cubed watermelon to the salad
ingredients used above. Toast 2 tablespoons
sunflower seeds and sprinkle over the salad
before serving.

celery, red onion & potato salad

Serves **4**
Preparation time **10 minutes**
Cooking time **10–15 minutes**

500 g (1 lb) **new potatoes**,
  halved
1 **small fennel bulb**, halved,
  cored and finely sliced
2 **celery sticks**, thinly sliced
1 **red onion**, halved and
  thinly sliced
celery leaves or **dill sprigs**,
  to garnish (optional)

For the mayonnaise dressing
150 ml (¼ pint) **mayonnaise**
2 teaspoons **wholegrain
  mustard**
2 tablespoons finely
  chopped **dill**
salt and pepper

Cook the potatoes in a large saucepan of salted boiling water for 10–15 minutes or until tender.

Meanwhile, combine the fennel, celery and onion in a large, shallow bowl. To make the dressing, mix all the ingredients together in a small bowl and season to taste with salt and pepper.

Drain the potatoes, rinse under cold running water, then drain again. Add the potatoes to the salad. Add the dressing and toss until well coated. Garnish with celery leaves or dill sprigs, if liked, before serving.

For herbed vinaigrette dressing, as a fresh, fragrant alternative to the mayonnaise dressing above, put 4 tablespoons olive oil, 1 tablespoon chopped parsley, 1 tablespoon chopped basil, 1 teaspoon grated lemon rind and 1 tablespoon white wine vinegar in a screw-top jar with salt and pepper to taste and shake well. Toss with the vegetables as directed above, and garnish with a few torn basil leaves.

gado gado salad

Serves **4**
Preparation time **15 minutes**
Cooking time **10 minutes**

For the salad

4 **eggs**

1 **iceberg lettuce**, finely
shredded

2 **carrots**, peeled and cut into
matchsticks

½ **cucumber**, peeled and cut
into matchsticks

½ **red pepper**, cored,
deseeded and cut into
matchsticks

For the peanut dressing

4 tablespoons **crunchy
peanut butter**

juice of 1 **lime**

1 tablespoon **clear honey**

1 tablespoon **soy sauce**

½ teaspoon finely chopped
red chilli

Put the eggs in a saucepan of cold water and bring
to the boil. Cook for 10 minutes, then plunge into
cold water to cool. Shell the eggs, then cut them in
half lengthways.

Combine all the remaining salad ingredients in a bowl,
then add the egg halves.

Put all the dressing ingredients in a saucepan and heat
gently, stirring, until combined. Drizzle the dressing over
the salad and serve immediately or serve the dressing
as a dipping sauce for the salad.

For gado gado with noodles & tofu to serve as
an impressive main course, cook 300 g (10 oz) dried
fine egg noodles in a saucepan of boiling water for
4 minutes or until just tender while the eggs are
cooking as in step 1 above. Drain and refresh the
noodles under cold running water. Spread over the
base of a shallow serving platter. Pat 125 g (4 oz) firm
tofu dry with kitchen paper, then cut into bite-sized
cubes. Heat a shallow depth of groundnut oil in a
frying pan, add the tofu cubes and cook over a high
heat until crisp and browned all over. Remove with a
slotted spoon and drain on kitchen paper. Assemble
the salad as above, spoon on top of the noodles and
scatter with the tofu. Drizzle over the dressing and
serve warm.

soft boiled egg & bacon salad

Serves **4**
Preparation time **10 minutes**
Cooking time **10 minutes**

4 thick slices of **day-old
  bread**
6 tablespoons **olive oil**
4 **eggs**
1 tablespoon **Dijon mustard**
juice of ½ **lemon**
100 g (3½ oz) **streaky bacon,**
  cut into bite-sized pieces
100 g (3½ oz) **rocket leaves**
salt and pepper

Cut the bread into small bite-sized pieces and toss in 2 tablespoons of the oil. Spread out on a baking sheet and bake in a preheated oven, 200°C (400°F), Gas Mark 6, for 10 minutes or until golden brown.

Meanwhile, cook the eggs in a saucepan of boiling water for 4 minutes. Drain, then cool under cold running water for 1 minute.

Whisk together the remaining oil, mustard and lemon juice in a small bowl.

Heat a nonstick frying pan, add the bacon and cook over a medium heat for 5 minutes until crisp and golden. Put into a bowl with the rocket.

Shell the eggs, then roughly break in half and add to the bacon and rocket. Scatter over the croûtons, then drizzle over the dressing, season to taste with salt and pepper and serve immediately.

For creamy yogurt dressing, to drizzle over the salad instead of the mustard dressing, whisk together 4 tablespoons olive oil, the juice of 1 lemon, 6 tablespoons natural yogurt, 1 crushed garlic clove, 1 teaspoon clear honey and 1 teaspoon dried oregano.

rice & pasta

tomato & bacon rice

Serves **4**
Preparation time **10 minutes**,
   plus standing
Cooking time **about**
   20 minutes

2 tablespoons **olive oil**
2 **large leeks**, sliced
1 **garlic clove**, crushed
200 g (7 oz) **back bacon**,
   chopped
400 g (13 oz) can **chopped**
   tomatoes
250 g (8 oz) **long-grain rice**
750 ml (1¼ pints) **chicken**
   stock
salt and pepper
chopped **flat leaf parsley**,
   to garnish

Heat the oil in a saucepan, add the leeks, garlic and bacon and cook over a medium heat for a few minutes until soft and starting to brown. Add the tomatoes and rice and cook, stirring, for 1 minute.

Add the stock and season to taste with salt and pepper. Reduce the heat, cover tightly and cook for 12–15 minutes or until all the stock has been absorbed and the rice is tender.

Remove from the heat and leave to stand, covered, for 10 minutes. Stir, then garnish with parsley and serve immediately.

For homemade chicken stock, chop a cooked chicken carcass into 3–4 pieces and put in a large saucepan with 1 chopped onion, 2–3 chopped carrots, 1 chopped celery stick, 1 bay leaf, 3–4 parsley stalks and 1 thyme sprig. Add 1.8 litres (3 pints) cold water and bring to the boil, skimming any scum that rises to the surface. Reduce the heat and simmer gently for 2–2½ hours. Strain through a muslin-lined sieve. If not using straight away, leave to cool before covering and refrigerating.

mustard & ham macaroni cheese

Serves **4**
Preparation time **5 minutes**
Cooking time **15 minutes**

350 g (11½ oz) **dried quick-
cook macaroni**
250 g (8 oz) **mascarpone
cheese**
100 g (3½ oz) **Cheddar
cheese**, grated
100 ml (3½ fl oz) **milk**
2 teaspoons **Dijon mustard**
400 g (13 oz) can **premium
cured ham**, cut into small
cubes
salt and pepper
chopped **flat leaf parsley**,
to garnish

Cook the macaroni in a large saucepan of salted
boiling water according to the packet instructions until
al dente, then drain and put in a warmed serving bowl.
Cover and keep warm.

Gently heat the mascarpone, Cheddar, milk and
mustard in a saucepan until melted into a sauce. Stir in
the ham and cook gently for 1–2 minutes. Season to
taste with salt and pepper.

Serve the macaroni with the cheese sauce spooned
over, garnished with chopped parsley.

For spinach with olive oil & lemon dressing, an
ideal accompaniment to the above dish, rinse 625 g
(1¼ lb) spinach leaves in cold water, then put in a
large saucepan with just the water that is clinging to
the leaves, sprinkling with salt to taste. Cover and
cook over a medium heat for 5–7 minutes until wilted
and tender, shaking the pan vigorously from time to
time. Drain thoroughly in a colander, then return to the
rinsed-out pan and toss over a high heat until any
remaining water has evaporated. Add 2 tablespoons
butter and 2 finely chopped garlic cloves, and
continue tossing until combined with the spinach.
Transfer to a warmed serving dish, drizzle over
4 tablespoons olive oil and 2 tablespoons lemon
juice, season to taste with salt and pepper and serve
immediately with the macaroni dish.

pasta with aubergines & pine nuts

Serves **4**
Preparation time **10 minutes**
Cooking time **15 minutes**

8 tablespoons **olive oil**

2 **aubergines**, diced

2 **red onions**, sliced

75 g (3 oz) **pine nuts**

3 **garlic cloves**, crushed

5 tablespoons **sun-dried tomato paste**

150 ml (¼ pint) **vegetable stock**

300 g (10 oz) **cracked pepper-, tomato- or mushroom-flavoured fresh ribbon pasta**

100 g (3½ oz) **pitted black olives**

salt and pepper

3 tablespoons roughly chopped **flat leaf parsley**, to garnish

Heat the oil in a large frying pan, add the aubergines and onions and cook for 8–10 minutes until tender and golden. Add the pine nuts and garlic and cook, stirring, for 2 minutes. Stir in the sun-dried tomato paste and stock and simmer for 2 minutes.

Meanwhile, cook the pasta in a large saucepan of salted boiling water for 2 minutes or until al dente.

Drain the pasta and return to the pan. Add the vegetable mixture and olives, season to taste with salt and pepper and toss together over a medium heat for 1 minute until combined. Serve scattered with the chopped parsley.

For potato-topped aubergine & tomato casserole, cook 4 potatoes in a large saucepan of salted boiling water until just tender. Meanwhile, follow the first stage of the recipe above, but omit the pine nuts, and add just 2 tablespoons sun-dried tomato paste together with 3 large skinned and chopped tomatoes and the stock. Simmer for 5 minutes, then slice the olives and stir into the mixture. Transfer to a shallow ovenproof dish. Drain the potatoes, cut into slices and arrange, overlapping, on top of the vegetable mixture. Sprinkle with 4 tablespoons finely grated Parmesan cheese and bake in a preheated oven, 200°C (400°F), Gas Mark 6, for 35–40 minutes until golden brown on top.

creamy blue cheese pasta

Serves **4**
Preparation time **10 minutes**
Cooking time **10 minutes**

375 g (12 oz) **dried
  pasta shells**
2 tablespoons **olive oil**
6 **spring onions**, thinly sliced
150 g (5 oz) **dolcelatte
  cheese**, diced
200 g (7 oz) **cream cheese**
salt and pepper
3 tablespoons chopped
  chives, to garnish

Cook the pasta shells in a large saucepan of salted boiling water according to the packet instructions until al dente.

Meanwhile, heat the oil in a large frying pan, add the spring onions and cook over a medium heat for 2–3 minutes. Add the cheeses and stir while they blend into a smooth sauce.

Drain the pasta shells and transfer to a warmed serving bowl. Stir in the sauce and season to taste with salt and pepper. Sprinkle with the chives and serve immediately.

For cheese & leek filo parcels, fry 3 leeks, thinly sliced, until soft and starting to brown, then leave to cool. Mix with the cheeses as above and 3 tablespoons chives. Melt 75 g (3 oz) butter in a saucepan. Put 8 sheets of filo pastry on a plate and cover with a damp tea towel. Working with 1 pastry sheet at a time, cut into 3 equal strips and brush well with melted butter. Put a teaspoon of the cheese mixture at one end of each strip. Fold one corner diagonally over to enclose and continue folding to the end of the strip to make a triangular parcel. Brush with melted butter and lay on a baking sheet. Repeat with the remaining cheese mixture and pastry to make about 24 small parcels. Bake in a preheated oven, 220°C (425°F), Gas Mark 7, for 8–10 minutes until golden brown. Serve hot.

tuna & sweetcorn pilaff

Serves **4**
Preparation time **10 minutes**
Cooking time **15–20 minutes**

2 tablespoons **olive oil**
1 **onion**, chopped
1 **red pepper**, cored,
   deseeded and diced
1 **garlic clove**, crushed
250 g (8 oz) **easy-cook
   long-grain rice**
750 ml (1¼ pints) **chicken
   stock**
325 g (11 oz) can **sweetcorn**,
   drained
200 g (7 oz) can **tuna in
   spring water**, drained
salt and pepper
6 chopped **spring onions**,
   to garnish

Heat the oil in a saucepan, add the onion, red pepper and garlic and cook until soft. Stir in the rice, then add the stock and season to taste with salt and pepper.

Bring to the boil, then reduce the heat and simmer, stirring occasionally, for 10–15 minutes until all the stock has been absorbed and the rice is tender.

Stir in the sweetcorn and tuna and cook briefly over a low heat to heat through. Serve immediately garnished with the spring onions.

For picnic pilaff cake, put the cooked rice mixture in a 23 cm (9 inch) square nonstick cake tin. In a bowl, beat 4 eggs with 4 tablespoons finely chopped parsley, season well with salt and pepper and pour over the rice mixture. Bake in a preheated oven, 180°C (350°F), Gas Mark 4, for 25–30 minutes or until set. Leave to cool, then remove from the tin and serve cut into thick wedges.

summer vegetable fettuccine

Serves **4**
Preparation time **10 minutes**
Cooking time **15 minutes**

250 g (8 oz) **asparagus**,
   trimmed and cut into 5 cm
   (2 inch) lengths
125 g (4 oz) **sugarsnap peas**
400 g (13 oz) **dried
   fettuccine or pappardelle**
200 g (7 oz) **baby courgettes**
150 g (5 oz) **button
   mushrooms**
1 tablespoon **olive oil**
1 **small onion**, finely chopped
1 **garlic clove**, finely chopped
4 tablespoons **lemon juice**
2 teaspoons chopped
   tarragon
2 teaspoons chopped **parsley**
100 g (3½ oz) **smoked
   mozzarella cheese**, diced
salt and pepper

Cook the asparagus and sugarsnap peas in a saucepan of boiling water for 3–4 minutes, then drain and refresh under cold running water. Drain well and set aside.

Cook the pasta in a large saucepan of salted boiling water according to the packet instructions until al dente.

Meanwhile, halve the courgettes lengthways and cut the mushrooms in half. Heat the oil in a large frying pan, add the onion and garlic and cook for 2–3 minutes. Add the courgettes and mushrooms and cook, stirring, for 3–4 minutes. Stir in the asparagus and sugarsnap peas and cook for 1–2 minutes before adding the lemon juice and herbs.

Drain the pasta and return to the pan. Add the vegetable mixture and mozzarella and season to taste with salt and pepper. Toss gently to mix and serve.

For cheesy garlic bread to serve with the pasta, cut a baguette into 2.5 cm (1 inch) thick slices, cutting almost through to the bottom crust but keeping the slices together at the base. In a bowl, beat 125 g (4 oz) softened butter with 1 crushed garlic clove, 1½ tablespoons finely chopped parsley and 125 g (4 oz) finely grated Parmesan cheese. Spread the butter on either side of the bread slices and over the top of the loaf. Wrap tightly in foil, place on a baking sheet and bake in a preheated oven, 190°C (375°F), Gas Mark 5, for 15 minutes. Carefully open up the foil and fold back, then bake for a further 5 minutes. Cut into slices and serve hot.

carrot, pea & broad bean risotto

Serves **4**
Preparation time **15 minutes**
Cooking time **about
  25 minutes**

4 tablespoons **butter**
2 tablespoons **olive oil**
1 **large onion**, finely chopped
2 **carrots**, finely chopped
2 **garlic cloves**, finely
  chopped
350 g (11½ oz) **risotto rice**
200 ml (7 fl oz) **white wine**
1.5 litres (2½ pints) **vegetable
  stock**, heated to simmering
200 g (7 oz) **frozen peas**,
  defrosted
100 g (3½ oz) **frozen broad
  beans**, defrosted and peeled
50 g (2 oz) **Parmesan
  cheese**, finely grated
1 handful of **flat leaf parsley**,
  roughly chopped
salt and pepper

Melt the butter with the oil in a saucepan, add the onion, carrots and garlic and cook for about 3 minutes until soft. Add the rice and stir until coated with the butter mixture. Add the wine and cook rapidly, stirring, until it has evaporated.

Add the hot stock, a ladleful at a time, and cook, stirring constantly, until each addition has been absorbed before adding the next. Continue until all the stock has been absorbed and the rice is creamy and cooked but still retains a little bite – this will take around 15 minutes.

Add the peas and broad beans and heat through for 3–5 minutes. Remove from the heat and stir in the Parmesan and parsley. Season to taste with salt and pepper and serve immediately.

For Italian-style risotto balls, leave the risotto to cool, then chill overnight in the refrigerator. Form the chilled mixture into walnut-sized balls. Beat 2 eggs together in a shallow bowl. Roll the rice balls through the egg, then in 100 g (3½ oz) dried breadcrumbs to coat. Fill a deep, heavy-based saucepan one-third full with vegetable oil and heat to 180–190°C (350–375°F) or until a cube of bread browns in 30 seconds. Add the rice balls, in batches, and cook for 2–3 minutes until golden. Remove with a slotted spoon, drain on kitchen paper and serve.

red pepper & cheese tortellini

Serves **4**
Preparation time **10 minutes**,
   plus cooling
Cooking time **15 minutes**

2 **red peppers**
2 **garlic cloves**, chopped
8 **spring onions**, finely sliced
500 g (1 lb) **fresh cheese-
   stuffed tortellini or any
   other fresh stuffed
   tortellini of your choice**
175 ml (6 fl oz) **olive oil**
25 g (1 oz) **Parmesan
   cheese**, finely grated
salt and pepper

Cut the peppers into large pieces, removing the cores and seeds. Lay skin-side up under a preheated grill and cook until the skin blackens and blisters. Transfer to a plastic bag, tie the top to enclose and leave to cool, then peel away the skin.

Place the peppers and garlic in a food processor and blend until fairly smooth. Stir in the spring onions and set aside.

Cook the tortellini in a large saucepan of boiling water according to the packet instructions until al dente. Drain and return to the pan.

Toss the pepper mixture into the pasta and add the oil and Parmesan. Season to taste with salt and pepper and serve immediately.

For warm ham & red pepper tortellini salad, grill and peel the red peppers as above, then thinly slice. While the tortellini is cooking, thinly slice 1 red onion. Drain the pasta and toss with 125 g (4 oz) chopped cooked ham, 200 g (7 oz) rocket leaves and the onion and red peppers. Serve immediately.

lemon & chilli prawn linguine

Serves **4**
Preparation time **15 minutes**
Cooking time **about
  10 minutes**

375 g (12 oz) **dried linguine
  or spaghetti**
15 g (½ oz) **butter**
1 tablespoon **olive oil**
1 **garlic clove**, finely chopped
2 **spring onions**, thinly sliced
2 **red chillies**, deseeded and
  thinly sliced
450 g (14½ oz) **frozen large
  peeled prawns**, defrosted
2 tablespoons **lemon juice**
2 tablespoons finely chopped
  coriander leaves
salt and pepper

Cook the pasta in a large saucepan of salted boiling
water according to the packet instructions until al
dente. When the pasta is about half cooked, melt the
butter with the oil in a large nonstick frying pan. Add
the garlic, spring onions and chillies and cook, stirring,
for 2–3 minutes.

Add the prawns and cook briefly until heated through.
Pour in the lemon juice and stir in the coriander until
well mixed, then remove from the heat and set aside.

Drain the pasta and toss it with the prawn mixture,
either in the frying pan (if large enough) or in a large,
warmed serving bowl. Season well with salt and pepper
and serve immediately.

For lime & chilli squid noodles, slit the bodies of
450 g (14½ oz) small squid down one side and lay flat
on a board, insides up. Using a sharp knife, score the
flesh with a criss-cross pattern. Cut any tentacles into
small pieces. Cook 375 g (12 oz) dried medium egg
noodles in a saucepan of boiling water according to
the packet instructions until just tender. Meanwhile,
heat 2 tablespoons groundnut oil in a large nonstick
frying pan or wok, add 2 thinly sliced garlic cloves
and a 2.5 cm (1 inch) piece of fresh root ginger,
peeled and chopped, together with the spring onions
and chillies as above, and stir-fry over a high heat for
2 minutes. Add the squid and stir-fry for 2–3 minutes.
Add the juice of 1 lime, 2 tablespoons dark soy sauce,
1 tablespoon Thai fish sauce and 2 tablespoons finely
chopped coriander leaves, stir briefly, then remove
from the heat. Drain the noodles, toss with the squid
mixture and serve immediately.

pasta with tomato & basil sauce

Serves **4**
Preparation time **10 minutes**
Cooking time **10 minutes**

400 g (13 oz) **dried spaghetti**
5 tablespoons **olive oil**
5 **garlic cloves**, finely
   chopped
6 **vine-ripened tomatoes**,
   deseeded and chopped
25 g (1 oz) **basil leaves**
salt and pepper

Cook the pasta in a large saucepan of salted boiling water according to the packet instructions.

Meanwhile, heat the oil in a frying pan, add the garlic and cook over a low heat for 1 minute. As soon as the garlic begins to change colour, remove the pan from the heat and add the remaining oil.

Drain the pasta and return to the pan. Add the garlic oil with the chopped tomatoes and basil leaves. Season to taste with salt and pepper and toss well to mix. Serve immediately.

For quick tomato & basil pizza, prepare the garlic oil as above, but use 4 tablespoons oil and 4 garlic cloves. Meanwhile, skin the tomatoes and deseed and chop them as above. Pour off half the oil and reserve, add the tomatoes and half the basil to the pan, season well and leave to simmer while you make the dough. Sift 250 g (8 oz) self-raising flour and 1 teaspoon salt into a large bowl, then gradually add 150 ml (¼ pint) warm water, mixing well to form a soft dough. Work the dough into a ball with your hands. Knead on a lightly floured surface until smooth and soft. Roll out the dough to a 30 cm (12 inch) round, making the edge slightly thicker than the centre, and lay on a warmed baking sheet. Spread the tomato mixture over the dough base, top with 125 g (4 oz) sliced mozzarella cheese and drizzle with the remaining garlic oil. Bake in a preheated oven, 240°C (475°F), Gas Mark 9, for 15 minutes or until the base is golden. Scatter with the remaining basil leaves and serve immediately.

courgette & herb risotto

Serves **4**
Preparation time **10 minutes**
Cooking time **about
    20 minutes**

4 tablespoons **butter**
2 tablespoons **olive oil**
1 **large onion**, finely chopped
2 **garlic cloves**, finely
    chopped
350 g (11½ oz) **risotto rice**
200 ml (7 fl oz) **white wine**
1.5 litres (2½ pints) **vegetable
    ·stock**, heated to simmering
200 g (7 oz) **baby leaf
    spinach**, chopped
100 g (3½ oz) **courgettes**,
    finely diced
50 g (2 oz) **Parmesan
    cheese**, finely grated
1 small handful of **dill, mint
    and chives**, roughly
    chopped
salt and pepper

Melt the butter with the oil in a saucepan, add the
onion and garlic and cook for about 3 minutes until
soft. Add the rice and stir until coated with the butter
mixture. Add the wine and cook rapidly, stirring, until it
has evaporated.

Add the hot stock, a ladleful at a time, and cook,
stirring constantly, until each addition has been
absorbed before adding the next. Continue until all the
stock has been absorbed and the rice is creamy and
cooked but still retains a little bite – this will take
around 15 minutes.

Stir in the spinach and courgettes and heat through for
3–5 minutes. Remove from the heat and stir in the
Parmesan and herbs. Season to taste with salt and
pepper and serve immediately.

For courgette & carrot risotto, cook the onion and
garlic in the butter and oil as above, but add 2 finely
chopped celery sticks and 3 small diced carrots.
Continue with the recipe above until the end of the
second stage. Meanwhile, cut 3 courgettes into
1 cm (½ inch) cubes. Add the courgettes to the risotto
and heat through for 3–5 minutes. Remove from the
heat and stir in 1 tablespoon chopped basil with the
Parmesan. Season to taste with salt and pepper and
serve immediately.

mixed bean kedgeree

Serves **4**
Preparation time **10 minutes**
Cooking time **15–20 minutes**

2 tablespoons **olive oil**
1 **onion**, chopped
2 tablespoons **mild curry powder**
250 g (8 oz) **long-grain rice**
750 ml (1¼ pints) **vegetable stock**
4 **eggs**
2 x 400 g (13 oz) cans **mixed beans**, drained and rinsed
150 ml (¼ pint) **soured cream**
salt and pepper
2 **tomatoes**, finely chopped, to garnish
flat leaf parsley, to garnish

Heat the oil in a saucepan, add the onion and cook until soft. Stir in the curry powder and rice. Add the stock and season to taste with salt and pepper. Bring to the boil, then reduce the heat, cover and simmer, stirring occasionally, for 10–15 minutes until all the stock has been absorbed and the rice is tender.

Meanwhile, put the eggs in a saucepan of cold water and bring to the boil. Cook for 10 minutes, then plunge into cold water to cool. Shell the eggs, then cut them into wedges.

Stir through the beans and soured cream and cook briefly over a low heat to heat through. Serve garnished with the eggs, tomatoes and parsley.

For chicken & pineapple pilaff, follow the first stage of the recipe above, but stir in 2 teaspoons turmeric with the curry powder and use chicken stock in place of the vegetable stock. Stir 400 g (13 oz) chopped cooked chicken breast and a 250 g (8 oz) can pineapple pieces in natural juice, drained, into the rice with the soured cream and cook briefly over a low heat to heat through. Serve garnished with 3 tablespoons chopped coriander leaves.

pappardelle puttanesca

Serves **4**
Preparation time **10 minutes**
Cooking time **15 minutes**

2 tablespoons **olive oil**
1 **onion**, chopped
2 **red chillies**, deseeded and
   finely chopped
2 **garlic cloves**, crushed
1 tablespoon **capers**
2 x 400 g (13 oz) cans
   chopped tomatoes
100 g (3½ oz) **pitted**
   black olives
50 g (2 oz) can **anchovy**
   fillets in oil, drained
400 g (13 oz) **dried**
   pappardelle or fettuccine
25 g (1 oz) **Parmesan**
   cheese, finely grated
salt and pepper

Heat the oil in a saucepan, add the onion, chillies and garlic and cook until soft. Add the capers, tomatoes, olives and anchovies, cover tightly and simmer for 10 minutes. Season to taste with salt and pepper.

Meanwhile, cook the pasta in a large saucepan of salted boiling water according to the packet instructions until al dente.

Drain the pasta. Serve immediately topped with the sauce and the Parmesan.

For tuna & olive pasta sauce, cook the onion and garlic as above but with ½ teaspoon dried red chilli flakes instead of the chillies. Then, in place of the anchovies, add a 200 g (7 oz) can tuna in oil, drained and flaked, to the pan with the capers, tomatoes and olives. Simmer for 10 minutes, then stir in 200 ml (7 fl oz) half-fat crème fraîche and season to taste with salt and pepper just before serving on top of the drained pasta. Scatter with the Parmesan and 1 tablespoon finely chopped parsley.

pasta pie

Serves **4**
Preparation time **10 minutes**
Cooking time **30 minutes**

1 tablespoon **olive oil**
450 g (14½ oz) **leeks**, sliced
2 **garlic cloves**, crushed
4 **eggs**, beaten
150 ml (¼ pint) **single cream**
125 g (4 oz) **Gruyère cheese**,
   grated
125 g (4 oz) **cooked fusilli**
salt and pepper

Heat the oil in a frying pan, add the leeks and garlic and cook until soft.

Mix the leek mixture with all the remaining ingredients, season to taste with salt and pepper and transfer to a greased ovenproof dish or medium-sized cake tin.

Bake in a preheated oven, 180°C (350°F), Gas Mark 4, for 25 minutes or until the eggs have set and the pie is golden brown. Serve with a crisp green salad.

For chicken & mozzarella macaroni pie, follow the first stage of the recipe, then add 200 g (7 oz) cooked chicken, cut into small bite-sized pieces, and 2 tablespoons finely chopped tarragon with the eggs and cream, together with 125 g (4 oz) grated mozzarella cheese and 125 g (4 oz) cooked macaroni. Bake in the oven as above.

meat & poultry

pea & lamb korma

Serves **4**

Preparation time **10 minutes**

Cooking time **30 minutes**

2 tablespoons **olive oil**

1 **onion**, chopped

2 **garlic cloves**, crushed

250 g (8 oz) **potatoes**, cut into 1.5 cm (¾ inch) dice

500 g (1 lb) **minced lamb**

1 tablespoon **korma curry powder**

200 g (7 oz) **frozen peas**

200 ml (7 fl oz) **vegetable stock**

2 tablespoons **mango chutney**

salt and pepper

chopped **coriander leaves**, to garnish

Heat the oil in a saucepan, add the onion and garlic and cook for 5 minutes until the onion is soft and starting to brown. Add the potatoes and minced lamb and cook, stirring and breaking up the mince with a wooden spoon, for 5 minutes or until the meat has browned.

Add the curry powder and cook, stirring, for 1 minute. Add the remaining ingredients and season to taste with salt and pepper. Bring to the boil, then reduce the heat, cover tightly and simmer for 20 minutes.

Remove from the heat, garnish with chopped coriander and serve with natural yogurt and steamed rice.

For spicy Indian wraps, finely shred 200 g (7 oz) iceberg lettuce and place in a bowl with 1 coarsely grated carrot. Heat 8 large flour wraps (or tortillas) on a griddle pan for 1–2 minutes on each side and then add the lettuce mixture on to the centre of each one. Divide the korma mixture (cooked as above) between the wraps and roll each one to enclose the filling. Serve accompanied with a dollop of yogurt if liked.

thai green pork curry

Serves **4**
Preparation time **10 minutes**
Cooking time **20 minutes**

2 tablespoons **olive oil**
4 **boneless pork steaks**, cut
   into bite-sized pieces
2 tablespoons **Thai green
   curry paste** (see page 196)
400 ml (14 fl oz) **coconut
   milk**
100 g (3½ oz) **green beans**
200 g (7 oz) can **water
   chestnuts**, drained, rinsed
   and cut in half
juice of **1 lime**, or to taste
1 handful of **coriander leaves**

Heat the oil in a large saucepan, add the pork and cook, stirring, for 3–4 minutes until browned all over. Add the curry paste and cook, stirring, for 1 minute until fragrant.

Add the coconut milk, stir and reduce the heat to a gentle simmer. Cook for 10 minutes, then add the beans and water chestnuts. Cook for a further 3 minutes.

Remove from the heat, add lime juice to taste and stir through the coriander. Serve immediately with boiled rice.

For Thai red pork curry, replace the Thai green curry paste with Thai red curry paste. To prepare your own Thai red curry paste, put 10 large red chillies, 2 teaspoons coriander seeds, 5 cm (2 inch) piece of fresh root ginger, peeled and finely chopped, 1 finely chopped lemon grass stalk, 4 halved garlic cloves, 1 roughly chopped shallot, 1 teaspoon lime juice and 2 tablespoons groundnut oil in a food processor or blender and process to a thick paste. Alternatively, pound the ingredients together using a pestle and mortar. Transfer the paste to an airtight container; it can be stored in the refrigerator for up to 3 weeks.

chicken ratatouille

Serves **2**

Preparation time **15 minutes**

Cooking time **25 minutes**

2 tablespoons **olive oil**

2 **boneless, skinless chicken breasts**, cut into bite-sized pieces

65 g (2½ oz) **courgettes**, thinly sliced

75 g (3 oz) **aubergine**, cubed

150 g (5 oz) **onion**, thinly sliced

50 g (2 oz) cored, deseeded **green pepper**, thinly sliced

75 g (3 oz) **mushrooms**, sliced

400 g (13 oz) can **plum tomatoes**

2 **garlic cloves**, finely chopped

1 teaspoon **organic vegetable bouillon powder**

1 teaspoon **dried basil**

1 teaspoon **dried parsley**

½ teaspoon **ground black pepper**

Heat the oil in a large frying pan, add the chicken and cook, stirring, for 3–4 minutes until browned all over. Add the courgettes, aubergine, onion, green pepper and mushrooms and cook, stirring occasionally, for 15 minutes or until tender.

Add the tomatoes to the pan and gently stir. Stir in the garlic, bouillon powder, herbs and pepper and simmer, uncovered, for 5 minutes or until the chicken is tender. Serve immediately.

For roasted potatoes with rosemary and garlic, to serve as an accompaniment, heat 2 tablespoons olive oil in a large roasting tin in a preheated oven, 230°C (450°F), Gas Mark 8. Meanwhile, cut 750 g (1½ lb) scrubbed, unpeeled potatoes into quarters lengthways and pat dry with kitchen paper. Mix together 2 tablespoons olive oil and 2 tablespoons chopped rosemary in a bowl, add the potatoes and toss to coat. Add to the roasting tin, shake carefully to form an even layer, then roast at the top of the oven for 20 minutes. Meanwhile, peel and thinly slice 4 garlic cloves. Remove the tin and move the potatoes around so that they cook evenly. Scatter the garlic slices among the potatoes, then return to the oven and cook for a further 5 minutes. Season to taste with salt and pepper and serve immediately with the chicken ratatouille.

moroccan meatball tagine

Serves **4**
Preparation time **15 minutes**
Cooking time **40 minutes**

2 small **onions**, finely chopped
2 tablespoons **raisins**
750 g (1½ lb) **minced beef**
1 tablespoon **tomato purée**
3 teaspoons **curry powder**
3 tablespoons **olive oil**
½ teaspoon **ground cinnamon**
625 g (1¼ lb) can
  chopped tomatoes
juice of ½ **lemon**
2 **celery sticks**, thickly sliced
1 large or 2 medium
  courgettes, roughly
  chopped
175 g (6 oz) **frozen peas**

Mix together half the onions, the raisins, minced beef, tomato purée and curry powder in a bowl. Using your hands, knead to combine the mixture evenly. Form the mixture into 24 meatballs.

Heat 1 tablespoon of the oil in a saucepan, add the meatballs, in small batches, and cook until browned all over. Tip out the excess fat and put all the meatballs in the pan. Add the cinnamon, tomatoes and lemon juice, cover and simmer gently for 25 minutes until the meatballs are cooked.

Meanwhile, heat the remaining oil in a large frying pan, add the celery and courgettes and cook until soft and starting to brown. Add the peas and cook for a further 5 minutes until the peas are tender.

Just before serving, stir the courgette mixture into the meatball mixture.

For coriander & apricot couscous, to serve as an accompaniment, put 200 g (7 oz) instant couscous in a large, heatproof bowl with 50 g (2 oz) chopped ready-to-eat dried apricots. Pour over boiling hot vegetable stock to just cover the couscous. Cover and leave to stand for 10–12 minutes until all the water has been absorbed. Meanwhile, chop 2 large, ripe tomatoes and finely chop 2 tablespoons coriander leaves. Fluff up the couscous grains with a fork and tip into a warmed serving dish. Stir in the tomatoes and coriander with 2 tablespoons olive oil and season to taste with salt and pepper. Toss well to mix and serve with the tagine.

spicy pork rolls with minted yogurt

Serves **4**
Preparation time **15 minutes**
Cooking time **10–12 minutes**

4 **pork escalopes**, about
125–150 g (4–5 oz) each
1 **small onion**, roughly
chopped
1 **red chilli**, deseeded and
roughly chopped
4 tablespoons roughly
chopped **coriander leaves**
grated rind and juice of 1 **lime**
1 tablespoon **Thai fish sauce**
2 **garlic cloves**, crushed
1 teaspoon grated **fresh
root ginger**
1 teaspoon **ground cumin**
½ teaspoon **ground coriander**
50 ml (2 fl oz) **coconut milk**
mint leaves, to garnish
(optional)

For the minted yogurt
200 ml (7 fl oz) **Greek yogurt**
4 tablespoons roughly
chopped **mint leaves**
salt and pepper

Lay a pork escalope between 2 sheets of clingfilm and pound lightly with a mallet until about 5 mm (¼ inch) thick. Repeat with the remaining escalopes.

Process the remaining ingredients in a food processor or blender to a coarse paste. Spread a quarter of the paste over a pork escalope and roll up to enclose the filling. Secure the roll with a wooden cocktail stick. Repeat with the remaining paste and pork.

Put the rolls on a baking sheet and cook in a preheated oven, 200°C (400°F), Gas Mark 6, for 10–12 minutes or until cooked through.

Meanwhile, to make the minted yogurt, put the yogurt in a small bowl, stir in the mint and season to taste with salt and pepper. Serve the rolls hot, with a dollop of the minted yogurt on the side and garnished with mint leaves, if liked.

For satay sauce to serve with the pork rolls instead of the minted yogurt, heat 1 tablespoon groundnut oil in a small frying pan, add 1 crushed garlic clove and cook, stirring, over a low heat for 2–3 minutes until softened. Stir in 4 tablespoons crunchy peanut butter, ¼ teaspoon dried chilli flakes, 1 tablespoon dark soy sauce, 1 tablespoon lime juice, 1 teaspoon clear honey and 2 tablespoons coconut cream and heat gently, stirring, until boiling. Serve warm with the pork rolls.

fast chicken curry

Serves **4**
Preparation time **5 minutes**
Cooking time **20–25 minutes**

3 tablespoons **olive oil**
1 **onion**, finely chopped
4 tablespoons **medium
  curry paste**
8 **chicken thighs**, boned,
  skinned and cut into
  thin strips
400 g (13 oz) can **chopped
  tomatoes**
250 g (8 oz) **broccoli**, broken
  into small florets, and stalks
  peeled and sliced
100 ml (3½ fl oz) **coconut
  milk**
salt and pepper

Heat the oil in a deep nonstick saucepan, add the onion and cook for 3 minutes until soft. Add the curry paste and cook, stirring, for 1 minute.

Add the chicken, tomatoes, broccoli and coconut milk to the pan. Bring to the boil, then reduce the heat, cover and cook over a low heat for 15–20 minutes.

Remove from the heat, season well with salt and pepper and serve immediately.

For seafood patties with curry sauce, follow the first stage of the recipe above, then add the tomatoes, 200 g (7 oz) young spinach leaves and the coconut milk and cook as directed. Meanwhile, put 375 g (12 oz) roughly chopped white fish fillets and 175 g (6 oz) frozen cooked peeled prawns, defrosted and roughly chopped, in a food processor and process until well combined. Alternatively, finely chop and mix together by hand. Transfer to a bowl, add 4 finely chopped spring onions, 2 tablespoons chopped coriander leaves, 50 g (2 oz) fresh white breadcrumbs, a squeeze of lemon juice, 1 beaten egg, and salt and pepper to taste. Mix well, then form into 16 patties. Roll in 25 g (1 oz) fresh white breadcrumbs to coat. Heat a shallow depth of vegetable oil in a large frying pan, add the patties, in batches, and cook for 5 minutes on each side or until crisp and golden brown. Serve hot with the curry sauce.

chicken thighs with fresh pesto

Serves **4**
Preparation time **15 minutes**
Cooking time **25 minutes**

1 tablespoon **olive oil**
8 **chicken thighs**
chopped basil leaves, to
   garnish

For the pesto
6 tablespoons **olive oil**
50 g (2 oz) **pine nuts**, toasted
50 g (2 oz) freshly grated
   Parmesan
50 g (2 oz) **basil leaves**
15 g (½ oz) **parsley**
2 **garlic cloves**, chopped
salt and pepper

Heat the oil in a nonstick frying pan over a medium heat. Add the chicken thighs and cook gently, turning frequently until the chicken is cooked through (about 20 minutes).

Meanwhile, make the pesto by placing all the ingredients in a food processor or blender and whizzing until smooth and well combined.

Remove the chicken from the pan and keep hot. Reduce the heat and add the pesto to the pan. Heat through for 2–3 minutes.

Pour the warmed pesto over the chicken thighs, garnish with basil and serve with courgette ribbons and grilled tomatoes.

For tomato rice as an accompaniment, cut 400 g (13 oz) cherry tomatoes in half and place on a nonstick baking tray. Sprinkle with 2 tablespoons of finely chopped garlic and sea salt and pepper to taste. Place in a hot oven for 12–15 minutes, then transfer to a mixing bowl with 250 g (8 oz) cooked basmati or long grain rice. Toss well to mix and serve with the chicken cooked as above.

134

bobotie

Serves **4**

Preparation time **10 minutes**, plus cooling

Cooking time **40 minutes**

2 tablespoons **olive oil**
1 **onion**, chopped
2 **garlic cloves**, chopped
2 tablespoons **medium curry paste**
500 g (1 lb) **minced beef**
2 tablespoons **tomato purée**
1 tablespoon **white wine vinegar**
50 g (2 oz) **sultanas**
1 slice of **white bread**, soaked in 3 tablespoons milk and mashed
4 **eggs**, beaten
100 ml (3½ fl oz) **double cream**
salt and pepper

Heat the oil in a saucepan, add the onion and garlic and cook until soft and starting to brown. Add the curry paste and minced beef and cook, stirring and breaking up with a wooden spoon, for 5 minutes or until browned.

Add the tomato purée, vinegar, sultanas and mashed bread. Season to taste with salt and pepper and transfer to a deep, medium-sized ovenproof dish or a 20 cm (8 inch) heavy cake tin.

Mix together the eggs and cream in a bowl, season to taste with salt and pepper and pour over the meat mixture.

Bake in a preheated oven, 180°C (350°F), Gas Mark 4, for 30 minutes or until the egg is set and golden brown. Remove from the oven and leave to cool for 10–15 minutes before serving.

For individual boboties to serve as a stylish starter for an elegant dinner, divide the meat mixture between 4 individual ramekin dishes and pour the egg mixture over each one. Bake in a preheated oven, 180°C (350°F), Gas Mark 4, for 20–25 minutes or until the tops are just set. Meanwhile, toast thin slices of bread in a preheated griddle pan or under a preheated grill. Serve with the boboties.

pesto turkey kebabs

Serves **4**

Preparation time **15 minutes**

Cooking time **about
12 minutes**

4 **turkey breast steaks**, about
   500 g (1 lb) in total
2 tablespoons **pesto**
4 slices of **Parma ham**
125 g (4 oz) **sun-dried
   tomatoes**, finely chopped
125 g (4 oz) **mozzarella
   cheese**, finely diced
1 tablespoon **olive oil**
salt and pepper
chopped parsley, to garnish
lemon wedges, to serve

Lay a turkey steak between 2 sheets of clingfilm and pound lightly with a mallet until about 1 cm (½ inch) thick. Repeat with the remaining steaks.

Spread the pesto over each beaten turkey steak and lay 1 slice of Parma ham on top of each. Sprinkle the tomatoes and mozzarella evenly over the turkey steaks, then season to taste with salt and pepper and roll up each one from the long side.

Cut the turkey rolls into 2.5 cm (1 inch) slices. Carefully thread the slices of roll evenly on to 4 metal skewers.

Brush the turkey rolls lightly with the oil and grill under a preheated grill for 6 minutes on each side or until cooked through. Increase or reduce the temperature setting of the grill, if necessary, to ensure that the rolls cook through and brown on the outside. Garnish with chopped parsley and serve hot with lemon wedges for squeezing over.

For homemade pesto, put 50 g (2 oz) pine nuts and 2 crushed garlic cloves in a food processor or blender and process to a thick paste. Alternatively, put in a mortar and pound with a pestle. Tear 50 g (2 oz) basil leaves into shreds and process or pound to a thick paste. Transfer both pastes to a bowl. Stir in 150 g (5 oz) finely grated Parmesan cheese and 2 tablespoons lemon juice. Add 150 ml (¼ pint) olive oil a little at a time, beating well. Season to taste with salt and pepper.

coconut chicken

Serves **4**
Preparation time **10 minutes**
Cooking time **20 minutes**

1 tablespoon **vegetable oil**
1 **onion**, diced
1 **red pepper**, cored,
  deseeded and diced
8 **chicken thighs**, boned,
  skinned and cut into bite-
  sized pieces
200 g (7 oz) **mangetout**
2 tablespoons **medium
  curry paste**
1 teaspoon finely chopped
  lemon grass stalks
1 teaspoon finely chopped
  fresh root ginger
2 **garlic cloves**, crushed
1 tablespoon **soy sauce**
400 ml (14 fl oz) **coconut
  milk**
1 handful of **basil leaves**
salt and pepper (optional)

Heat the oil in a saucepan, add the onion and red pepper and cook for 5 minutes until soft and just starting to brown. Add the chicken and cook for 5 minutes until browned all over.

Add the mangetout, curry paste, lemon grass, ginger, garlic and soy sauce and cook, stirring, for 2–3 minutes. Add the coconut milk and stir well. Cover and simmer gently for 5–8 minutes.

Remove from the heat, check and adjust the seasoning if necessary and stir in the basil just before serving with boiled basmati rice.

For spicy fried rice to serve as an alternative accompaniment, heat 2 tablespoons vegetable oil in a wok or large frying pan and crack 2 eggs into it, breaking the yolks and stirring them around. Add 250 g (8 oz) cold, cooked long-grain rice, 3 teaspoons caster sugar, 1½ tablespoons soy sauce, 2 teaspoons crushed dried chillies and 1 teaspoon Thai fish sauce and stir-fry over a high heat for 2 minutes. Serve immediately with the coconut chicken, garnished with coriander leaves.

duck breasts with fruity salsa

Serves **4**
Preparation time **15 minutes**
Cooking time **about
  15 minutes**

2 large **boneless duck
  breasts**, skin on, halved
  lengthways
2 tablespoons **dark soy
  sauce**
1 tablespoon **clear honey**
1 teaspoon grated **fresh
  root ginger**
1 teaspoon **chilli powder**

For the fruity salsa
1 large ripe **mango**, peeled,
  stoned and finely diced
6–8 **plums**, stoned and
  finely diced
grated rind and juice of **1 lime**
1 small **red onion**, finely
  chopped
1 tablespoon **olive oil**
1 tablespoon roughly chopped
  mint leaves
1 tablespoon roughly chopped
  coriander leaves
salt and pepper

Use a sharp knife to score the skin on the duck
breasts lightly, cutting down into the fat but not through
to the meat.

Heat a frying pan until very hot, then add the duck
breasts, skin-side down, and cook for 3 minutes or until
sealed and browned. Turn over and cook for 2 minutes.
Use a slotted spoon to transfer the duck breasts to a
baking sheet, skin-side up.

In a small bowl, mix together the soy sauce, honey,
ginger and chilli powder. Spoon over the duck. Cook
in a preheated oven, 200°C (400°F), Gas Mark 6, for
6–9 minutes, until cooked to your liking. The duck may
be served pink in the centre or more well cooked.

Meanwhile, in a bowl, mix together all the ingredients
for the salsa and season well with salt and pepper.

Thinly slice the cooked duck and fan out the slices
slightly on individual plates. Spoon some of the salsa
over the duck and serve immediately, offering the
remaining salsa separately.

For apricot & lime salsa as an alternative to the plum
and mango salsa, in a bowl mix together 250 g (8 oz)
drained and finely chopped canned apricots in natural
juice, the grated rind and juice of 1 lime, 1 finely
chopped shallot, 1 tablespoon finely chopped fresh
root ginger, 1 tablespoon olive oil and 2 teaspoons
clear honey.

rice noodles with lemon chicken

Serves **4**
Preparation time **10 minutes**
Cooking time **10 minutes**

4 **boneless chicken breasts**,
  skin on
juice of 2 **lemons**
4 tablespoons **sweet
  chilli sauce**
250 g (8 oz) **dried rice
  noodles**
1 small bunch of **flat leaf
  parsley**, chopped
1 small bunch of **coriander**,
  chopped
½ **cucumber**, peeled into
  ribbons with a vegetable
  peeler
salt and pepper
finely chopped **red chilli**,
  to garnish

Mix the chicken with half the lemon juice and the
sweet chilli sauce in a large bowl and season to taste
with salt and pepper.

Lay a chicken breast between 2 sheets of clingfilm and
lightly pound with a mallet to flatten. Repeat with the
remaining chicken breasts.

Arrange the chicken on a grill rack in a single layer.
Cook under a preheated grill for 4–5 minutes on each
side or until cooked through. Finish on the skin side so
that it is crisp.

Meanwhile, put the noodles in a heatproof bowl, pour
over boiling water to cover and leave for 10 minutes
until just tender, then drain. Add the remaining lemon
juice, herbs and cucumber to the noodles and toss well
to mix. Season to taste with salt and pepper.

Top the noodles with the cooked chicken and serve
immediately, garnished with the chopped red chilli.

For stir-fried ginger broccoli to serve as an
accompaniment, trim the stalks from 500 g (1 lb)
broccoli. Divide the heads into florets, then diagonally
slice the stalks. Blanch the florets and stalks in a
saucepan of salted boiling water for 30 seconds.
Drain, refresh under cold running water and drain
again thoroughly. Heat 2 tablespoons vegetable oil in
a large frying pan, add 1 thinly sliced garlic clove and
a 2.5 cm (1 inch) piece of fresh root ginger, peeled
and finely chopped, and stir-fry for a few seconds.
Add the broccoli and stir-fry over a high heat for
2 minutes. Sprinkle over 1 teaspoon sesame oil and
stir-fry for a further 30 seconds.

quick sausage & bean casserole

Serves **4**
Preparation time **5 minutes**
Cooking time **25 minutes**

2 tablespoons **olive oil**
16 **cocktail sausages**
2 **garlic cloves**, crushed
400 g (13 oz) can **chopped tomatoes**
400 g (13 oz) can **baked beans**
200 g (7 oz) can **mixed beans**, drained and rinsed
½ teaspoon **dried thyme**
salt and pepper
3 tablespoons chopped **flat leaf parsley**, to garnish

Heat the oil in a frying pan, add the sausages and cook until browned all over.

Transfer the sausages to a large saucepan and add all the remaining ingredients. Bring to the boil, then reduce the heat, cover tightly and simmer for 20 minutes. Season to taste with salt and pepper and serve hot, garnished with the chopped herbs.

For mustard mash to serve as an accompaniment, cook 1 kg (2 lb) chopped potatoes in a large saucepan of salted boiling water until tender. Drain well and return to the pan. Mash with 75 g (3 oz) butter, 1 tablespoon wholegrain mustard, 3 teaspoons prepared English mustard and 1 crushed garlic clove. Season to taste with salt and pepper, then beat in 2 tablespoons chopped parsley and a dash of olive oil. Serve hot with the casserole.

jerk chicken wings

Serves **4**
Preparation time **5 minutes**,
  plus marinating
Cooking time **12 minutes**

12 large **chicken wings**
2 tablespoons **olive oil**
1 tablespoon **jerk
  seasoning mix**
juice of ½ **lemon**
1 teaspoon **salt**
chopped **flat leaf parsley**,
  to garnish
lemon wedges, to serve

Put the chicken wings in a glass or ceramic dish. In a small bowl, whisk together the oil, jerk seasoning mix, lemon juice and salt, pour over the wings and stir well until evenly coated. Cover and leave to marinate in the refrigerator for at least 30 minutes or overnight.

Arrange the chicken wings on a grill rack and cook under a preheated grill, basting halfway through cooking with any remaining marinade, for 6 minutes on each side or until cooked through, tender and lightly charred at the edges. Increase or reduce the temperature setting of the grill, if necessary, to ensure that the wings cook through. Garnish with the chopped parsley and serve immediately with lemon wedges for squeezing over.

For jerk lamb kebabs, coat 750 g (1½ lb) boneless lamb, cut into bite-sized pieces in the jerk marinade as above, leaving to marinate overnight if time allows. Thread the meat on to 8 metal skewers and cook under a preheated grill or over a barbecue for 6–8 minutes on each side or until cooked to your liking.

pork & red pepper chilli

Serves **4**
Preparation time **10 minutes**
Cooking time **30 minutes**

2 tablespoons **olive oil**
1 large **onion**, chopped
2 **garlic cloves**, crushed
1 **red pepper**, cored,
   deseeded and diced
450 g (14½ oz) **minced pork**
1 **red chilli**, finely chopped
1 teaspoon **dried oregano**
500 g (1 lb) **passata (sieved
   tomatoes)**
400 g (13 oz) can **red kidney
   beans**, drained and rinsed
salt and pepper
soured cream, to serve

Heat the oil in a saucepan, add the onion, garlic and red pepper and cook for 5 minutes until soft and starting to brown. Add the minced pork and cook, stirring and breaking up with a wooden spoon, for 5 minutes or until browned.

Add all the remaining ingredients and bring to the boil. Reduce the heat and simmer gently for 20 minutes. Remove from the heat, season well with salt and pepper and serve immediately with a dollop of soured cream and boiled rice or crusty bread.

For lamb & aubergine chilli, substitute the pork mince and red pepper with 1 medium aubergine and 450 g (14½ oz) lamb mince. Cut the aubergine into small cubes and fry as above with the lamb mince. Garnish the finished dish with 2 tablespoons of finely chopped mint leaves and serve with rice or pasta.

teriyaki chicken

Serves **4**
Preparation time **10 minutes**,
  plus marinating
Cooking time **8 minutes**

2 **boneless, skinless chicken
  breasts**, cut into thin strips
2 tablespoons **soy sauce**
1 tablespoon **olive oil**
2 **large carrots**, peeled and
  cut into small matchsticks
2 **red peppers**, cored,
  deseeded and cut into small
  matchsticks
200 g (7 oz) jar **teriyaki
  stir-fry sauce**
6 **spring onions**, chopped

Put the chicken in a glass or ceramic bowl, add the soy sauce and toss well to coat. Cover and leave to marinate in a cool place for 10 minutes.

Heat the oil in a wok or large frying pan, add the chicken and marinade and stir-fry for 2 minutes. Add the carrots and peppers and stir-fry for 4 minutes. Add the sauce and spring onions and cook briefly, stirring, to heat through. Serve immediately over egg noodles.

For pork teriyaki with crispy garlic, substitute the chicken with 625 g (1¼ lb) pork steaks. Place the steaks between sheets of clingfilm and flatten with a wooden mallet. Cut into thin strips and cook as above. To make the crispy garlic, thinly slice 4 garlic cloves. Heat a 5 cm (2 inch) depth of oil in a deep, heavy-based saucepan to 180–190°C (350–375°F) or until a cube of bread browns in 30 seconds. Add the garlic slices and cook until golden and crispy. Remove with a slotted spoon and drain on kitchen paper. Sprinkle over the finished dish.

beef with black bean sauce

Serves **4**
Preparation time **15 minutes**
Cooking time **15 minutes**

750 g (1½ lb) **minute steak**
2 tablespoons **groundnut oil**
1 **onion**, thinly sliced
100 g (3½ oz) **mangetout**,
  halved lengthways
1 **garlic clove**, finely chopped
15 g (½ oz) **fresh ginger root**,
  peeled and finely chopped
1 small **red chilli**, finely
  chopped
200 g (7 oz) jar **black
  bean sauce**
salt and pepper

Trim the steak of all fat and then cut the meat into thin slices across the grain. Heat half the oil in a wok or large frying pan, add the beef, in 2 batches, and cook, stirring, until well browned all over. Transfer to a bowl.

Heat the remaining oil in the pan, add the onion and mangetout and stir-fry for 2 minutes. Add the garlic, ginger and chilli and stir-fry for 1 minute. Add the black bean sauce and cook, stirring, for 5 minutes or until the sauce begins to thicken. Season to taste with salt and pepper and serve immediately with steamed rice or egg-fried rice.

For seafood with black bean sauce, stir-fry 500 g (1 lb) raw tiger prawns and 200 g (7 oz) squid rings in a hot wok for 2–3 minutes. Add 8 roughly sliced spring onions and 2 sliced red peppers and stir-fry for a further 2–3 minutes. Add the black bean sauce and cook for 5 minutes, stirring often. Serve hot with egg noodles.

tandoori chicken

Serves **4**

Preparation time **5 minutes**,
    plus marinating

Cooking time **25–30 minutes**

8 **chicken drumsticks**

8 **chicken thighs**

2 tablespoons **tikka spice
    mix or paste**

2 **garlic cloves**, crushed

1 tablespoon **tomato purée**

juice of 1 **lemon**

75 ml (3 fl oz) **natural yogurt**

To garnish

grated lime rind

chopped coriander

Make deep slashes all over the chicken pieces. In
a large glass or ceramic bowl, mix together all the
remaining ingredients, then add the chicken and turn
to coat thoroughly with the marinade. Cover and leave
to marinate in the refrigerator for at least 30 minutes
or overnight.

Transfer the chicken to an ovenproof dish and cook
in a preheated oven, 240°C (475°F), Gas Mark 9, for
25–30 minutes until cooked through, tender and lightly
charred at the edges. Serve garnished with lime rind
and chopped coriander.

For blackened tandoori salmon, use the marinade
above to coat 4 thick, skinless salmon fillets, then
cover and leave to marinate in the refrigerator for
30 minutes–1 hour. Transfer to a nonstick baking
sheet and bake at 180°C (350°F), Gas Mark 4, for
20 minutes or until cooked through. Serve with plain
rice or couscous.

griddled salsa chicken

Serves **4**
Preparation time **10 minutes**
Cooking time **6 minutes**

4 **boneless chicken breasts**,
  skin on
3 tablespoons **olive oil**
salt and pepper

For the cucumber and
tomato salsa
1 **red onion**, finely chopped
2 **tomatoes**, deseeded
  and diced
1 **cucumber**, finely diced
1 **red chilli**, finely chopped
1 small handful of **coriander**
  leaves, chopped
juice of 1 **lime**

Remove the skin from the chicken breasts. Using kitchen scissors, cut each breast in half lengthways but without cutting the whole way through. Open each breast out flat. Brush with the oil and season well with salt and pepper. Heat a griddle pan until very hot. Add the chicken breasts and cook for 3 minutes on each side or until cooked through and grill-marked.

Meanwhile, to make the salsa, mix together the onion, tomatoes, cucumber, red chilli, coriander and lime juice. Season well with salt and pepper.

Serve the chicken hot with the spicy salsa spooned over and around.

For griddled tuna with pineapple salsa, prepare and cook 4 thick fresh tuna steaks, about 175 g (6 oz) each, as for the butterflied chicken breasts above. Meanwhile, in a bowl, mix together 6 tablespoons drained and roughly diced canned pineapple, 1 finely chopped red onion, 1 tablespoon finely chopped fresh root ginger, 1 finely chopped red chilli, grated rind and juice of 1 lime, 2 teaspoons clear honey, and salt and pepper to taste. Serve the pineapple salsa with the griddled tuna.

chicken with spring herbs

Serves **4**
Preparation time **15 minutes**
Cooking time **20 minutes**

250 g (8 oz) **mascarpone cheese**
1 handful of **chervil**, finely chopped
½ bunch of **parsley**, finely chopped
2 tablespoons chopped **mint leaves**
4 **boneless chicken breasts**, skin on
200 ml (7 fl oz) **white wine**
25 g (1 oz) **butter**
salt and pepper

Mix together the mascarpone and herbs in a bowl and season well with salt and pepper.

Lift the skin away from each chicken breast and spread a quarter of the mascarpone mixture on each breast. Replace the skin and smooth carefully over the mascarpone mixture. Season to taste with salt and pepper.

Place the chicken in a baking dish and pour the wine around it. Dot the butter over the chicken.

Roast in a preheated oven, 180°C (350°F), Gas Mark 4, for 20 minutes until the chicken is golden and crisp. Remove from the oven and serve with garlic bread.

For baby glazed carrots as an alternative accompaniment to garlic bread, melt 25 g (1 oz) butter in a saucepan, add 500 g (1 lb) young carrots, quartered lengthways, a pinch of sugar, and salt and pepper to taste. Pour over just enough water to cover and simmer gently for 15–20 minutes until the carrots are tender and the liquid has evaporated, adding 2 tablespoons orange juice towards the end of the cooking time. Serve with the chicken garnished with chopped parsley.

mexican pie

Serves **4**
Preparation time **10 minutes**
Cooking time **30 minutes**

2 tablespoons **olive oil**
1 **onion**, finely chopped
2 **garlic cloves**, crushed
2 **carrots**, diced
250 g (8 oz) **minced beef**
1 **red chilli**, finely chopped
400 g (13 oz) can **chopped
   tomatoes**
400 g (13 oz) can **red kidney
   beans**, drained and rinsed
50 g (2 oz) **tortilla chips**
100 g (3½ oz) **Cheddar
   cheese**, grated
salt and pepper
**chopped parsley or
   coriander**, to garnish

Heat the oil in saucepan, add the onion, garlic and carrots and cook until softened. Add the minced beef and chilli and cook, stirring and breaking up with a wooden spoon, for 5 minutes or until the meat has browned. Add the tomatoes and beans, mix well and season to taste with salt and pepper.

Transfer to an ovenproof dish, cover with the tortilla chips and sprinkle with the Cheddar. Bake in a preheated oven, 200°C (400°F), Gas Mark 6, for 20 minutes or until golden brown. Garnish with chopped parsley or coriander before serving.

For tortilla-wrapped chilli with guacamole, follow the first stage of the recipe above, but then cover and simmer on the hob for 20 minutes. Meanwhile, halve 2 large, ripe avocados lengthways and remove the stones. Scoop the flesh into a bowl, add 3 tablespoons lime juice and roughly mash. Add 125 g (4 oz) tomatoes, skinned, deseeded and chopped, 2 crushed garlic cloves, 40 g (1½ oz) chopped spring onions, 1 tablespoon finely chopped green chillies and 2 tablespoons chopped coriander leaves, mix well and season to taste with salt and pepper. Divide the chilli between 4 warmed flour tortillas and wrap up. Serve with the guacamole, and soured cream, if liked.

minted lamb skewers

Serves **4**
Preparation time **10 minutes**
Cooking time **10 minutes**

500 g (1 lb) **minced lamb**
2 teaspoons **curry powder**
6 tablespoons finely chopped
  mint leaves
salt and pepper

Mix together the minced lamb, curry powder and mint in a bowl and season to taste with salt and pepper. Using your hands, knead to combine the mixture evenly.

Divide the mixture into small sausages and thread evenly on to metal skewers. Cook under a preheated grill for 10 minutes, turning once. Serve hot with warmed naan bread, soured cream and a lime wedge. Sprinkle with chopped mint leaves and a little curry powder.

For cucumber raita to serve as an accompaniment, cut ½ large cucumber in half lengthways, scoop out and discard the seeds, then thinly slice each half. In a bowl, mix together with 250 ml (8 fl oz) natural yogurt, 1 tablespoon chopped mint leaves and 1 tablespoon chopped coriander leaves. Season to taste with salt and pepper. Toast 2 teaspoons cumin seeds in a dry frying pan until fragrant. Sprinkle over the raita just before serving.

fish &
shellfish

creamy garlic mussels

Serves **4**
Preparation time **15 minutes**
Cooking time **about
8 minutes**

1.5 kg (3 lb) **fresh, live
mussels**
1 tablespoon **butter**
1 **onion**, finely chopped
6 **garlic cloves**, finely
chopped
100 ml (3½ fl oz) **white wine**
150 ml (¼ pint) **single cream**
1 large handful of **flat leaf
parsley**, roughly chopped
salt and pepper

Scrub the mussels in cold water, scrape off any barnacles and pull away the dark hairy beards that protrude from the shells. Discard any with broken shells or any open mussels that do not close when tapped sharply.

Melt the butter in a large saucepan, add the onion and garlic and cook for 2–3 minutes until transparent and softened.

Increase the heat and tip in the mussels with the wine, then cover and cook for 3 minutes or until all the shells have opened. Discard any that remain closed.

Pour in the cream and heat through briefly, stirring well. Add the parsley, season well with salt and pepper and serve immediately in large bowls, with crusty bread to mop up the juices.

For mussels in spicy tomato sauce, cook the onion and garlic in 1 tablespoon olive oil instead of the butter, together with 1 deseeded and finely chopped red chilli. Add 1 teaspoon paprika and cook, stirring, for 1 minute, then add 400 g (13 oz) can chopped tomatoes. Season to taste with salt and pepper, cover and simmer gently for 15 minutes. Meanwhile, clean the mussels, as in the first stage above. Stir the mussels into the tomato sauce and increase the heat. Cover and cook for 3 minutes or until all the shells have opened. Discard any that remain closed. Add the parsley and serve as above.

sesame prawns with pak choi

Serves **4**
Preparation time **10 minutes**,
   plus marinating
Cooking time **about
   3 minutes**

600 g (1 lb 3 oz) **large frozen
   peeled prawns**, defrosted
1 teaspoon **sesame oil**
2 tablespoons **light soy
   sauce**
1 tablespoon **clear honey**
1 teaspoon grated **fresh
   root ginger**
1 teaspoon crushed **garlic**
1 tablespoon **lemon juice**
500 g (1 lb) **pak choi**
2 tablespoons **vegetable oil**
salt and pepper

Put the prawns in a glass or ceramic bowl. Add the sesame oil, soy sauce, honey, ginger, garlic and lemon juice. Season to taste with salt and pepper and mix well, then cover and leave to marinate in a cool place for 5–10 minutes.

Cut the heads of pak choi in half lengthways, then blanch in a large saucepan of boiling water for 40–50 seconds. Drain well, cover and keep warm.

Heat the vegetable oil in a wok or large frying pan. Add the prawns and marinade and stir-fry over a high heat for 2 minutes until thoroughly hot.

Divide the pak choi between 4 serving plates, then top with the prawns and any juices from the pan. Serve immediately.

For sesame chicken with broccoli & red pepper, use 600 g (1 lb 3 oz) boneless, skinless chicken breast, cut into thin strips, in place of the prawns. Coat with the marinade as above, then cover and leave to marinate in the refrigerator for 1–2 hours. Meanwhile, trim the stalks from 400 g (13 oz) broccoli. Divide the heads into small florets, then peel and diagonally slice the stalks. Blanch the florets and stalks in a large saucepan of salted boiling water for 30 seconds. Drain well, refresh under cold running water and drain again thoroughly. Core, deseed and thinly slice 1 large red pepper. Heat the oil in the wok or large frying pan as above, add the chicken and marinade and stir-fry over a high heat for 2 minutes. Add the broccoli and red pepper and stir-fry for a further 2 minutes. Serve immediately.

egg pots with smoked salmon

Serves **4**
Preparation time **5 minutes**
Cooking time **10–15 minutes**

200 g (7 oz) **smoked salmon trimmings**
2 tablespoons chopped **chives**
4 **eggs**
4 tablespoons **double cream**
toasted bread, to serve
pepper

Divide the smoked salmon and chives between 4 buttered ramekins. Make a small indent in the salmon with the back of a spoon and break an egg into the hollow, sprinkle with a little pepper and spoon the cream over the top.

Put the ramekins in a roasting tin and half-fill the tin with boiling water. Bake in a preheated oven, 180°C (350°F), Gas Mark 4, for 10–15 minutes or until the eggs have just set.

Remove from the oven and leave to cool for a few minutes, then serve with the toasted bread.

For homemade Melba toast, to serve with the baked egg pots, toast 4 slices of bread lightly on both sides. While hot, trim off the crusts, then split the toast in half widthways. Lay the toast, cut-side up, on a baking sheet and bake in the bottom of the oven with the egg pots until dry.

fish kebabs & spring onion mash

Serves **4**
Preparation time **15 minutes**,
   plus marinating
Cooking time **18–20 minutes**

600 g (1 lb 3 oz) **skinless
   haddock, cod or coley
   fillets**, cut into 2.5 cm
   (1 inch) cubes
125 ml (4 fl oz) **natural yogurt**
1 teaspoon crushed **garlic**
1 teaspoon grated **fresh
   root ginger**
1 teaspoon **hot chilli powder**
1 tablespoon **ground
   coriander**
1 tablespoon **ground cumin**

For the spring onion mash
6 large **Desirée or King
   Edward potatoes**, diced
150 ml (¼ pint) **crème fraîche**
4 tablespoons finely chopped
   coriander leaves
1 **red chilli**, deseeded and
   thinly sliced
4 **spring onions**, thinly sliced
salt and pepper

Lay the fish cubes in a large, shallow glass or ceramic dish. In a small bowl, mix together the yogurt, garlic, ginger, chilli powder, ground coriander and cumin. Season the mixture to taste and pour over the fish. Cover and leave to marinate in a cool place while you make the mash.

Cook the potatoes in a large saucepan of salted boiling water for 10 minutes or until tender. Drain in a colander and return to the pan. Mash the potatoes and add the crème fraîche. Continue mashing until smooth, then stir in the chopped coriander, chilli and spring onions. Season to taste with salt and pepper, cover and set aside.

Heat the grill on the hottest setting. Thread the cubes of fish evenly on to 4 metal skewers and cook under the grill for 8–10 minutes, turning once. Serve immediately, with the mash and a green salad.

For spinach mash, to serve as an alternative accompaniment, while the potatoes are cooking, heat 2 tablespoons oil in a saucepan, add 1 finely chopped onion and 1 finely chopped garlic clove and cook for 5 minutes. Add 500 g (1 lb) chopped spinach leaves and cook, stirring, for 2 minutes or until the spinach just starts to wilt. Stir in 1 teaspoon ground ginger. Mash the potatoes with the spinach mixture and 4 tablespoons milk. Season to taste with salt and pepper.

mackerel with avocado salsa

Serves **4**
Preparation time **10 minutes**
Cooking time **6–8 minutes**

8 mackerel fillets
2 **lemons**, plus extra wedges
  to serve
salt and pepper

For the avocado salsa
2 **avocados**, peeled, stoned
  and finely diced
juice and rind of 1 **lime**
1 **red onion**, finely chopped
½ **cucumber**, finely diced
1 handful of **coriander leaves**,
  finely chopped

Make 3 diagonal slashes across each mackerel fillet on the skin side and season well with salt and pepper. Cut the lemons in half, then squeeze the juice over the fish.

Lay on a grill rack, skin-side up, and cook under a preheated grill for 6–8 minutes or until the skin is lightly charred and the flesh is just cooked through.

Meanwhile, to make the salsa, mix together the avocados and lime juice and rind, then add the onion, cucumber and coriander. Toss well to mix and season to taste with salt and pepper.

Serve the mackerel hot with the avocado salsa and lemon wedges for squeezing over.

For grilled sardines with tomato relish, replace the mackerel fillets with 12 whole, cleaned and gutted sardines and grill for 4–5 minutes on each side. Meanwhile, put the chopped white parts of 4 spring onions, 2 tablespoons lime juice, 250 g (8 oz) ripe tomatoes, skinned, deseeded and chopped, ½ chopped sun-dried tomato, 1 deseeded and chopped red chilli and 3 tablespoons chopped coriander leaves in a food processor or blender and process until well combined. Serve the sardines hot with the relish.

salmon with lime courgettes

Serves **4**
Preparation time **10 minutes**
Cooking time **10–15 minutes**

4 **salmon fillet** portions, about
   200 g (7 oz) each
1 tablespoon prepared
   English mustard
1 teaspoon grated **fresh
   root ginger**
1 teaspoon crushed **garlic**
2 teaspoons **clear honey**
1 tablespoon **light soy sauce**
   or **tamari**
salt and pepper

For the lime courgettes
2 tablespoons **olive oil**
500 g (1 lb) **courgettes**, thinly
   sliced lengthways
grated rind and juice of **1 lime**
2 tablespoons chopped **mint**

Lay the salmon fillet portions, skin-side down, in a
shallow flameproof dish, to fit snugly in a single layer.
In a small bowl, mix together the mustard, ginger, garlic,
honey and soy sauce or tamari, then spoon evenly over
the fillets. Season to taste with salt and pepper.

Heat the grill on the hottest setting. Cook the salmon
fillets under the grill for 10–15 minutes, until lightly
charred on top and cooked through.

Meanwhile, to prepare the lime courgettes, heat the oil
in a large nonstick frying pan, add the courgettes and
cook, stirring frequently, for 5–6 minutes or until lightly
browned and tender. Stir in the lime rind and juice and
mint and season to taste with salt and pepper.

Serve the salmon hot with the courgettes.

For stir-fried green beans to serve in place of the
lime courgettes, cut 500 g (1 lb) green beans into
5 cm (2 inch) lengths. Heat 2 tablespoons vegetable
oil in a wok or large frying pan, add 2 crushed garlic
cloves, 1 teaspoon grated fresh root ginger and
2 thinly sliced shallots and stir-fry over a medium
heat for 1 minute. Add the beans and ½ teaspoon
salt and stir-fry over a high heat for 1 minute. Add
1 tablespoon light soy sauce and 150 ml (¼ pint)
chicken or vegetable stock and bring to the boil.
Reduce the heat and cook, stirring frequently, for a
further 4 minutes, or until the beans are tender and
the liquid has thickened. Season with pepper and
serve immediately with the salmon.

spiced calamari with parsley salad

Serves **4**

Preparation time **15 minutes**,
  plus standing

Cooking time **about
  5 minutes**

150 g (5 oz) **besan** (chickpea
  or gram flour)
1½ teaspoons **paprika**
1½ teaspoons **ground cumin**
½ teaspoon **baking powder**
¼ teaspoon **pepper**
250 ml (8 fl oz) **soda water**
vegetable oil, for deep-frying
6 **whole squid**, cleaned
  and cut into 1 cm (½ inch)
  thick rings
salt

For the parsley salad
4 tablespoons **lemon juice**
4 tablespoons **olive oil**
2 **garlic cloves**, finely
  chopped
20 g (¾ oz) **flat leaf parsley**
1 **red onion**, halved and
  thinly sliced
2 **tomatoes**, roughly chopped

Sift the besan, paprika, cumin and baking powder into a bowl, add the pepper and mix together. Make a well in the centre. Gradually add the soda water and whisk until it is a smooth batter. Season to taste with salt. Cover and leave to stand for 30 minutes.

Meanwhile, for the salad dressing, in a bowl, whisk together the lemon juice, olive oil and garlic.

Fill a deep, heavy-based saucepan one-third full with vegetable oil and heat until a cube of bread browns in 15 seconds. Dip the squid rings in the batter, add to the oil, in batches, and cook for 30–60 seconds until golden brown. Remove with a slotted spoon and drain on kitchen paper.

Add the parsley, red onion and tomatoes to the dressing and toss well to mix. Top with the battered squid and serve immediately.

For pan-fried squid with chilli, slit the bodies of the squid down one side and lay flat, inside up. Using a sharp knife, score the flesh with a criss-cross pattern. Cut any tentacles into small pieces. In a bowl, mix together 2 tablespoons olive oil, 3 crushed garlic cloves, 1 finely chopped red chilli and 4 tablespoons lemon juice. Add the squid, cover and leave to marinate in a cool place for 15 minutes. Remove the squid from the marinade. Heat 2 tablespoons olive oil in a large frying pan until just smoking, add the squid and season to taste with salt and pepper. Cook, stirring, over a high heat for 2–3 minutes until browned. Strain the marinade and stir into the pan with 2 tablespoons finely chopped flat leaf parsley.

prawn & crab cakes with chilli jam

Serves **4**
Preparation time **15 minutes**,
   plus cooling and chilling
Cooking time **15 minutes**

2 x 175 g (6 oz) cans **white
   crab meat**
grated rind and juice of **1 lime**
4 **spring onions**, chopped
1 **red chilli**, deseeded and
   finely chopped
1 teaspoon grated **fresh
   root ginger**
1 teaspoon crushed **garlic**
3 tablespoons chopped
   coriander leaves, plus extra
   leaves to garnish
3 tablespoons **mayonnaise**
125 g (4 oz) **fresh white
   breadcrumbs**
200 g (7 oz) **frozen cooked
   peeled prawns**, defrosted
salt and pepper
vegetable oil, for shallow-
   frying

For the chilli jam
2 **red chillies**, deseeded and
   finely diced
6 tablespoons **caster sugar**
2 tablespoons **water**

Put the crab meat, lime rind and juice, spring onions, chilli, ginger, garlic, coriander, mayonnaise and breadcrumbs in a food processor and process until well combined. Transfer the mixture to a bowl. Chop the prawns and fold into the mixture with salt and pepper to taste. Alternatively, the ingredients can be mixed together by hand. Cover and chill while making and cooling the chilli jam.

Put all the chilli jam ingredients in a small saucepan and heat gently until simmering. Cook for 4–5 minutes until the sugar has dissolved and the mixture has thickened slightly. Leave to cool.

Form the prawn mixture into 12 cakes.

Heat the oil in a large nonstick frying pan, add the cakes and cook for 3–4 minutes on each side or until golden. Drain on kitchen paper and serve immediately garnished with coriander leaves. Serve the chilli jam spooned over the cakes or separately. A crisp rocket salad or green salad is a good accompaniment.

For coconut coriander sauce to serve as an alternative to the chilli jam, put 250 ml (8 fl oz) coconut milk, 2 tablespoons smooth peanut butter, 2 finely chopped spring onions, white parts only, 1 crushed garlic clove, 1 finely chopped green chilli, 2 tablespoons chopped coriander leaves, 1 tablespoon lime juice and 1 teaspoon sugar in a food processor or blender and process until smooth.

trout with cucumber relish

Serves **4**
Preparation time **10 minutes**
Cooking time **10–12 minutes**

4 **rainbow trout**, cleaned
   and gutted
1 tablespoon **sesame oil**
crushed **Szechuan pepper**,
   to taste
salt

For the cucumber relish
1 **cucumber**, about 20 cm
   (8 inches) long
2 teaspoons **salt**
4 tablespoons **rice vinegar**
3 tablespoons **caster sugar**
1 **red chilli**, deseeded
   and sliced
3 cm (1¼ inch) piece
   fresh root ginger, peeled
   and grated
4 tablespoons **cold water**

To garnish
chopped chives
lemon wedges

Cut the cucumber in half lengthways, scoop out and discard the seeds and cut the flesh into 1 cm (½ inch) slices. Put in a glass or ceramic bowl. In a small bowl, put the salt, vinegar, sugar, chilli and ginger, add the water and mix well. Pour over the cucumber, cover and leave to marinate at room temperature while you cook the trout.

Brush the trout with the oil and season to taste with crushed Szechuan pepper and salt. Place the trout in a single layer on a grill rack and grill for 5–6 minutes on each side or until cooked through. Leave to rest for a few moments, then garnish with chopped chives and serve with the cucumber relish and lemon wedges.

For trout with ground almond dressing, brush the trout with 1 tablespoon olive oil and season to taste with salt and black pepper. While the trout is cooking as above, put 125 g (4 oz) ground almonds in a small saucepan over a medium heat and cook, stirring constantly, until lightly browned. Remove from the heat, add 6 tablespoons olive oil, 4 tablespoons lemon juice and 2 tablespoons chopped parsley, and season to taste with salt and pepper. Stir well, then return to the heat for 2 minutes. Pour the dressing over the cooked trout, garnish with parsley sprigs and serve immediately.

summer prawn & fish filo pie

Serves **4**
Preparation time **10 minutes**
Cooking time **20–25 minutes**

750 g (1½ lb) **skinless white fish fillets**
100 g (3½ oz) **frozen cooked peeled prawns**, defrosted
100 g (3½ oz) **frozen peas**, defrosted
grated rind and juice of 1 **lemon**
600 ml (1 pint) **bottled white sauce**
1 bunch of **dill**, chopped
8 sheets of **filo pastry**
melted butter, for brushing
salt and pepper

Cut the fish into large, bite-sized pieces and put in a bowl with the prawns and peas. Add the lemon rind and juice, stir in the white sauce and dill and season well with salt and pepper.

Tip the fish mixture into 4 individual gratin or pie dishes. Cover the surface of each pie with 2 sheets of filo pastry, scrunching up each sheet into a loosely crumpled ball. Brush the pastry with melted butter.

Bake in a preheated oven, 200°C (400°F), Gas Mark 6, for 20–25 minutes until the pastry is golden brown and the fish is cooked through.

For seafood & potato pie, prepare the fish mixture as above, but use 2 tablespoons chopped parsley in place of the dill. Put into a medium-sized ovenproof dish. Cook 800 g (1 lb 10 oz) chopped potatoes in a large saucepan of salted boiling water until tender. Meanwhile, put 2 large eggs in a separate saucepan and bring to the boil. Cook for 10 minutes, then plunge into cold water to cool. Shell the eggs and cut in half lengthways. Drain the potatoes and mash with 2 tablespoons butter. Season well with salt and pepper. Gently press the egg halves, at evenly spaced intervals, into the fish mixture, then spoon or pipe the mash over the fish mixture. Bake in a preheated oven, 200°C (400°F), Gas Mark 6, for 20–25 minutes or until the top is lightly golden.

creamy prawn curry

Serves **4**

Preparation time **10 minutes**

Cooking time **about**
  10 minutes

2 tablespoons **vegetable oil**
1 **onion**, halved and finely
  sliced
2 **garlic cloves**, finely sliced
2.5 cm (1 inch) piece of **fresh
  root ginger**, peeled and
  finely chopped
1 tablespoon **ground
  coriander**
1 tablespoon **ground cumin**
½ teaspoon **turmeric**
200 ml (7 fl oz) **coconut milk**
125 ml (4 fl oz) **vegetable
  stock**
600 g (1 lb 3 oz) **frozen large
  cooked peeled prawns**,
  defrosted
grated rind and juice of 1 **lime**
4 tablespoons finely chopped
  coriander leaves
salt and pepper

Heat the oil in a large saucepan, add the onion, garlic
and ginger and cook for 4–5 minutes. Add the ground
coriander, cumin and turmeric and cook, stirring, for
1 minute.

Pour in the coconut milk and stock and bring to the
boil. Reduce the heat and simmer for 2–3 minutes. Stir
in the prawns and lime rind and juice, then simmer for
2 minutes or until the prawns are heated through.

Stir in the chopped coriander and season well with salt
and pepper. Serve immediately with boiled basmati or
jasmine rice.

For spiced coconut rice to serve with the curry, rinse
375 g (12 oz) basmati rice in cold water until the
water runs clear. Drain and put in a large, heavy-based
saucepan. Dissolve 125 g (4 oz) chopped creamed
coconut in 750 ml (1¼ pints) boiling water and add to
the rice with a 7 cm (3 inch) piece of lemon grass
stalk, halved lengthways, 2 x 2.5 cm (1 inch) pieces
of cinnamon stick, 1 teaspoon salt, and pepper to
taste. Bring the rice to the boil, then cover and cook
for 10 minutes until almost all the liquid has been
absorbed. Turn off the heat and leave to stand for
10 minutes until the rice is tender. Fluff up with a fork
before serving with the curry.

red salmon & roasted vegetables

Serves **4**
Preparation time **10 minutes**
Cooking time **25 minutes**

1 **aubergine**, cut into
   bite-sized pieces
2 **red peppers**, cored,
   deseeded and cut into
   bite-sized pieces
2 **red onions**, quartered
1 **garlic clove**, crushed
4 tablespoons **olive oil**
pinch of **dried oregano**
200 g (7 oz) can **red salmon**,
   drained and flaked
100 g (3½ oz) **pitted black
   olives**
salt and pepper
basil leaves, to garnish

Mix together the aubergine, red peppers, onions and garlic in a bowl with the oil and oregano and season well with salt and pepper.

Spread the vegetables out in a single layer in a nonstick roasting tin and roast in a preheated oven, 220°C (425°F), Gas Mark 7, for 25 minutes or until the vegetables are just cooked.

Transfer the vegetables to a warmed serving dish and gently toss in the salmon and olives. Serve warm or at room temperature, garnished with basil leaves.

For rocket & cucumber couscous to serve with the salmon and vegetables, put 200 g (7 oz) instant couscous in a large, heatproof bowl. Season well with salt and pepper and pour over boiling hot water to just cover the couscous. Cover and leave to stand for 10–12 minutes until all the water has been absorbed. Meanwhile, finely chop 4 spring onions, halve, deseed and chop ½ cucumber and chop 75 g (3 oz) rocket leaves. Fluff up the couscous grains with a fork and tip into a warmed serving dish. Stir in the prepared ingredients with 2 tablespoons olive oil and 1 tablespoon lemon juice. Toss well to mix and serve with the salmon and vegetables.

tuna niçoise spaghetti

Serves **4**
Preparation time **10 minutes**
Cooking time **10 minutes**

4 **eggs**
350 g (11½ oz) **dried spaghetti**
3 x 200 g (7 oz) cans **tuna in brine**, drained
100 g (3½ oz) **green beans**, trimmed and blanched
50 g (2 oz) **kalamata olives**, pitted
100 g (3½ oz) **semi-dried tomatoes**
1 teaspoon grated **lemon rind**
2 tablespoons **lemon juice**
3 tablespoons **capers**
salt and pepper

Put the eggs in a saucepan of cold water and bring to the boil. Cook for 10 minutes, then plunge into cold water to cool. Shell the eggs, then roughly chop and set aside.

Meanwhile, cook the pasta in a large saucepan of salted boiling water according to the packet instructions until al dente.

Mix together the tuna, beans, olives, semi-dried tomatoes, lemon rind and juice and capers in a bowl. Season to taste with pepper.

Drain the pasta and return to the pan. Add the tuna mixture and gently toss to combine. Serve immediately garnished with the eggs.

For tuna, pea & sweetcorn rice cook 200 g (7 oz) easy-cook basmati rice in a large saucepan of lightly salted boiling water for 12–15 minutes or until tender. Drain, refresh under cold running water and drain again. Meanwhile, cook the eggs as above, then shell and cut into quarters. In a separate saucepan, cook 100 g (3½ oz) frozen sweetcorn and 100 g (3½ oz) frozen peas in salted boiling water for 5 minutes or until tender. Drain, refresh under cold running water and drain again. In a large bowl, mix together the rice, sweetcorn and peas, together with the tuna and olives, as above, and 2 tablespoons chopped basil. Whisk together 2 tablespoons lemon juice, 1 tablespoon olive oil and 1 crushed garlic clove, add to the rice and toss well to coat. Serve garnished with the egg quarters.

moroccan grilled sardines

Serves **4**

Preparation time **10 minutes**

Cooking time **6–8 minutes**

12 **sardines**, cleaned
  and gutted
2 tablespoons **harissa**
2 tablespoons **olive oil**
juice of 1 **lemon**
salt flakes and pepper
chopped coriander,
  to garnish
lemon wedges, to serve

Heat the grill on the hottest setting. Rinse the sardines and pat dry with kitchen paper. Make 3 deep slashes on both sides of each fish with a sharp knife.

Mix the harissa with the oil and lemon juice to make a thin paste. Rub into the sardines on both sides. Put the sardines on a lightly oiled baking sheet. Cook under the grill for 3–4 minutes on each side, depending on their size, or until cooked through. Season to taste with salt flakes and pepper and serve immediately garnished with coriander and with lemon wedges for squeezing over.

For baked sardines with pesto, line a medium ovenproof dish with 2 sliced tomatoes and 2 sliced onions. Prepare the sardines as above, then rub 4 tablespoons pesto over the fish and arrange in a single layer on top of the tomatoes and onions. Cover with foil and bake in a preheated oven, 200°C (400°F), Gas Mark 6, for 20–25 minutes or until the fish is cooked through.

thai-style coconut mussels

Serves **4**

Preparation time **20 minutes**

Cooking time **about 10 minutes**

2 kg (4 lb) **fresh, live mussels**

600 ml (1 pint) **vegetable stock**

400 ml (14 fl oz) **coconut milk**

grated rind and juice of 2 **limes**

2 **lemon grass stalks,** lightly bruised, plus extra stalks to garnish (optional)

1 tablespoon **Thai green curry paste**

3 **red chillies,** deseeded and finely sliced

4 tablespoons chopped **coriander leaves,** plus extra to garnish (optional)

2 **spring onions,** shredded

salt and pepper

1 **red chilli,** deseeded and chopped, to garnish (optional)

Scrub the mussels in cold water, scrape off any barnacles and pull away the hairy beards that protrude from the shells. Discard any with broken shells or any open mussels that do not close when tapped sharply.

Pour the stock and coconut milk into a large saucepan and bring to the boil. Stir in the lime rind and juice, lemon grass, curry paste, chillies, coriander and spring onions. Season to taste with salt and pepper.

Add the mussels, cover and return to the boil. Cook for 3–4 minutes or until all the mussels have opened. Discard any shells that remain closed. Use a slotted spoon to divide the mussels between 4 serving bowls and keep warm until ready to serve.

Bring the liquid to a vigorous boil and boil rapidly for 5 minutes or until reduced. Strain through a fine sieve, then ladle over the mussels. Garnish with chopped red chilli, chopped coriander leaves and lemon grass stalks.

For homemade Thai green curry paste, put 15 small green chillies, 4 halved garlic cloves, 2 finely chopped lemon grass stalks, 2 torn lime leaves, 2 chopped shallots, 50 g (2 oz) coriander leaves, stalks and roots, 2.5 cm (1 inch) piece of fresh root ginger, peeled and finely chopped, 2 teaspoons black peppercorns, 1 teaspoon pared lime rind, ½ teaspoon salt and 1 tablespoon groundnut oil into a food processor or blender and process to a thick paste. Alternatively, use a pestle and mortar to crush the ingredients, working in the oil at the end. Transfer the paste to an airtight container; it can be stored in a refrigerator for up to 3 weeks.

desserts

pineapple with lime & chilli syrup

Serves **4**
Preparation time **10 minutes**,
 plus cooling
Cooking time **10 minutes**

100 g (3½ oz) **caster sugar**
100 ml (3½ fl oz) **water**
3 **red chillies**
grated rind and juice of 1 **lime**
1 **baby pineapple**, halved or
 quartered, cored and cut into
 wafer-thin slices

Put the sugar in a saucepan with the water. Heat slowly until the sugar has dissolved, then add the chillies, bring to the boil and boil rapidly until the liquid becomes syrupy. Leave to cool.

Stir the lime rind and juice into the cooled syrup. Lay the pineapple slices on a plate and drizzle the syrup over. Serve chilled with a dollop of ice cream, if liked.

For pears with cinnamon syrup, peel 4 ripe pears, cut into quarters and remove the cores. Put in a saucepan, pour over water to cover and add the caster sugar as above, together with the grated rind and juice of 1 lemon, 1 cinnamon stick and 6 cloves. Simmer, turning occasionally, for 10 minutes or until tender. Remove the pears with a slotted spoon and set aside. Bring the liquid to the boil and boil rapidly until the liquid becomes syrupy. Leave to cool, then pour over the pears.

tipsy berry waffles

Serves **4**
Preparation time **5 minutes**
Cooking time **1–2 minutes**

15 g (½ oz) **butter**
250 g (8 oz) **mixed berries**,
  such as blueberries,
  blackberries and raspberries
1 tablespoon **caster sugar**
2 tablespoons **kirsch**
4 **waffles**
4 tablespoons **crème fraîche**

Melt the butter in a nonstick frying pan, add the berries, sugar and kirsch and cook over a high heat, stirring gently, for 1–2 minutes.

Meanwhile, toast or reheat the waffles according to the packet instructions. Put a waffle on each serving plate, spoon the berries over the waffles and top each portion with 1 tablespoon crème fraîche. Serve immediately.

For homemade waffles, sift 125 g (4 oz) plain flour, 1 teaspoon baking powder and a pinch of salt into a bowl. Make a well in the centre and gradually beat in 2 eggs and 150 ml (¼ pint) milk until the batter is thick and smooth. Just before cooking, beat in 3 tablespoons cooled melted butter. Heat a waffle iron and oil if necessary. Spoon in enough batter to give a good coating, close and cook for about 1 minute on each side. Lift the lid and remove the waffle. Repeat with the remaining batter.

apricot tartlets

Serves **4**
Preparation time **15 minutes**
Cooking time **20–25 minutes**

375 g (12 oz) **ready-rolled
  puff pastry**, defrosted
  if frozen
100 g (3½ oz) **marzipan**
12 canned **apricot halves**,
  drained
light muscovado sugar,
  for sprinkling
apricot jam, for glazing

Using a saucer as a template, cut 4 rounds from the pastry, each approximately 8 cm (3½ inches) in diameter. Score a line about 1 cm (½ inch) from the edge of each round with a sharp knife.

Roll out the marzipan to 2.5 mm (⅛ inch) thick and cut out 4 rounds to fit inside the scored circles. Lay the pastry rounds on a baking sheet, place a circle of marzipan in the centre of each and arrange 3 apricot halves, cut-side up, on top. Sprinkle a little sugar into each apricot.

Put the baking sheet on top of a second preheated baking sheet (this helps to crisp the pastry bases) and bake in a preheated oven, 200°C (400°F), Gas Mark 6, for 20–25 minutes until the pastry is puffed and browned and the apricots are slightly caramelized around the edges. While still hot, brush the tops with apricot jam to glaze. Serve immediately.

For banana tartlets with rum mascarpone, follow the recipe above, but use 2 thickly sliced bananas in place of the apricots. While the tartlets are baking, in a bowl, mix together 4 tablespoons mascarpone cheese, 2 tablespoons rum and 2 tablespoons light muscovado sugar. Spoon on top of the hot tartlets and serve immediately.

hot berry soufflés

Serves **4**
Preparation time **10 minutes**
Cooking time **15 minutes**

15 g (½ oz) **butter**
100 g (3½ oz) **caster sugar**
50 g (2 oz) **blackberries**
200 g (7 oz) **raspberries**
4 **large egg whites**
icing sugar, for dusting
(optional)

Use the butter to grease 4 x 200 ml (7 fl oz) ramekins and then coat evenly with a little of the caster sugar, tipping out the excess sugar. Set the ramekins on a baking sheet.

Purée the blackberries and raspberries in a food processor or blender, reserving a few of the berries to decorate, then pour the purée into a bowl. Alternatively, the berries can be rubbed through a fine sieve to make a smooth purée.

Whisk the egg whites until stiff but not dry in a large, perfectly clean bowl. Gradually sprinkle in the remaining caster sugar, whisking continuously, and continue whisking until the whites are stiff and shiny.

Gently fold the egg whites into the berry purée, then spoon the mixture into the prepared ramekins. Bake immediately in a preheated oven, 190°C (375°F), Gas Mark 5, for 15 minutes or until risen and golden.

Dust the soufflés with icing sugar and decorate with the reserved berries. Serve immediately, with custard or ice cream, if liked.

For homemade custard to serve as an accompaniment, gently heat 300 ml (½ pint) milk in a saucepan without boiling. Meanwhile, beat 2 egg yolks in a bowl with 1 tablespoon sugar and a few drops of vanilla extract, then pour the milk into the bowl, stirring constantly. Return the mixture to the pan and heat over a low heat, stirring constantly, until the custard thickens enough to coat the back of the spoon. Serve immediately with the soufflés.

strawberry cheesecake pots

Serves **4**

Preparation time **15 minutes**,
  plus cooling and chilling

Cooking time **5 minutes**

25 g (1 oz) **butter**

5 **digestive biscuits**

175 g (6 oz) **strawberries**

2 tablespoons **caster sugar**

250 g (8 oz) **mascarpone
  cheese**

4 tablespoons **double cream**

4 tablespoons **icing sugar**

grated rind and juice of
  1 **lemon**

Melt the butter in a small saucepan, then transfer to a food processor with the digestive biscuits and process to fine crumbs. Divide the mixture between 4 glasses and press into the base of each. Chill in the refrigerator.

Meanwhile, put the strawberries and caster sugar in a saucepan and cook, stirring, for 2–3 minutes, then leave to cool. In a bowl, mix together the mascarpone, cream, icing sugar and lemon rind and juice.

Fill the glasses with the mascarpone mixture and top each with the strawberries. Chill for 2–3 hours before serving.

For ginger raspberry cheesecake pots, follow the recipe above, but use gingernut biscuits in place of the digestive biscuits, raspberries instead of strawberries and Greek yogurt in place of the mascarpone. Sprinkle the top of each dessert with 1 teaspoon chopped stem ginger.

walnut & white chocolate cookies

Makes **about 25**
Preparation time **15 minutes,**
 plus cooling
Cooking time **12–15 minutes**

1 **egg**
150 g (5 oz) **soft light
 brown sugar**
2 tablespoons **caster sugar**
1 teaspoon **vanilla extract**
125 ml (4 fl oz) **vegetable oil**
65 g (2½ oz) **plain flour**
3 tablespoons **self-raising
 flour**
¼ teaspoon **ground cinnamon**
25 g (1 oz) **shredded
 coconut**
175 g (6 oz) **walnuts**, toasted
 and chopped
125 g (4 oz) **white
 chocolate chips**

Grease 2 baking sheets and line with nonstick baking paper. In a bowl, beat the egg and sugars together until light and creamy. Stir in the vanilla extract and oil. Sift in the flours and cinnamon, then add the coconut, walnuts and chocolate and mix well with a wooden spoon.

Form rounded tablespoonfuls of the mixture into balls and place on the prepared baking sheets, pressing the mixture together with your fingertips if it is crumbly. Bake in a preheated oven, 180°C (350°F), Gas Mark 4, for 12–15 minutes or until golden. Leave to cool slightly on the sheets, then transfer to a wire rack to cool completely.

For hazelnut & chocolate chip cookies, follow the recipe above but use ½ teaspoon ground ginger in place of the cinnamon, toasted and chopped hazelnuts instead of the walnuts and plain dark chocolate chips in place of the white.

fig & honey pots

Serves **4**

Preparation time **10 minutes**, plus chilling

6 **ripe fresh figs**, thinly sliced, plus 2 extra, cut into wedges, to decorate (optional)

450 ml (¾ pint) **Greek yogurt**

4 tablespoons **clear honey**

2 tablespoons chopped **pistachio nuts**

Arrange the fig slices snugly in the bottom of 4 glasses or glass bowls. Spoon the yogurt over the figs and chill in the refrigerator for 10–15 minutes.

Just before serving, drizzle 1 tablespoon honey over each dessert and sprinkle the pistachio nuts on top. Decorate with the wedges of fig, if liked.

For hot figs with honey, heat a griddle pan, add 8 whole ripe fresh figs and cook for 8 minutes, turning occasionally, until charred on the outside. Alternatively, cook under a preheated grill. Remove and cut in half. Divide between 4 plates, top each with a tablespoonful of Greek yogurt and drizzle with a little clear honey.

rhubarb slumps

Serves **4**
Preparation time **10 minutes**
Cooking time **20–25 minutes**

400 g (13 oz) **rhubarb**, cut
  into chunks
6 tablespoons **golden
  caster sugar**
grated rind and juice of
  1 orange
100 g (3½ oz) **oats**
6 tablespoons **double cream**
2 tablespoons **dark
  muscovado sugar**

Mix together the rhubarb, golden caster sugar and orange rind and half the juice in a bowl. Spoon the mixture into 4 individual ramekins.

Put the oats, cream, dark muscovado sugar and remaining orange juice in the bowl and mix together. Drop spoonfuls of the oat mixture all over the surface of the rhubarb mixture.

Set the ramekins on a baking sheet and bake in a preheated oven, 180°C (350°F), Gas Mark 4, for 20–25 minutes until the topping is browned. Serve hot.

For apple and blackberry crumbles, peel, core and chop 2 dessert apples, then mix with 100 g (3½ oz) blackberries, 6 tablespoons golden caster sugar and 1 tablespoon apple juice. Spoon into the ramekins as above. Sift 125 g (4 oz) plain flour into a bowl, add 50 g (2 oz) diced butter and rub in with the fingertips until the mixture resembles coarse breadcrumbs. Stir in 50 g (2 oz) dark muscovado sugar, 25 g (1 oz) bran flakes and 50 g (2 oz) chopped mixed nuts. Spoon the mixture over the fruit and flatten slightly with the back of a spoon. Bake as above until the topping is lightly golden.

chocolate chip cookies

Makes **16**
Preparation time **10 minutes,**
  plus cooling
Cooking time **15 minutes**

125 g (4 oz) **unsalted butter,**
  diced and softened
175 g (6 oz) **soft light**
  brown sugar
1 teaspoon **vanilla extract**
1 **egg**, lightly beaten
1 tablespoon **milk**
200 g (7 oz) **plain flour**
1 teaspoon **baking powder**
250 g (8 oz) **plain dark**
  chocolate chips

Line a large baking sheet with nonstick baking paper. In a large bowl, beat the butter and sugar together until light and fluffy. Mix in the vanilla extract, then gradually beat in the egg, beating well after each addition. Stir in the milk.

Sift the flour and baking powder into a separate large bowl, then fold into the butter and egg mixture. Stir in the chocolate chips.

Drop level tablespoonfuls of the cookie mixture on to the prepared baking sheet, leaving about 3.5 cm (1½ inches) between each cookie, then lightly press with a floured fork. Bake in a preheated oven, 180°C (350°F), Gas Mark 4, for 15 minutes or until lightly golden. Transfer to a wire rack to cool.

For chocolate & mandarin log, drain a 300 g (10 oz) can mandarin segments and finely chop, reserving a few whole segments for decoration. In a bowl, whip 300 ml (½ pint) double cream with 25 g (1 oz) icing sugar until thick, then fold in the chopped mandarins. Sandwich the cooked chocolate chip cookies one on top of the other with half the mandarin cream, then carefully set the log on its side and wrap in foil. Chill in the refrigerator for at least 2–3 hours or overnight. Just before serving, put the log on a serving plate, cover with the remaining mandarin cream and decorate with the reserved mandarins. Serve in slices, cut on the diagonal.

caramelized banana puff tart

Serves **4**
Preparation time **10 minutes**
Cooking time **15–20 minutes**

3 **bananas**, sliced
375 g (12 oz) **ready-made
  puff pastry**, defrosted
  if frozen
1 **egg**, beaten
3 tablespoons **unrefined
  demerara sugar**
300 ml (½ pint) **whipping
  cream** (optional)

Slice the bananas in half horizontally. Roll the pastry into a 20 cm (8 inch) square and cut the pastry into equal quarters. Place on a baking sheet and score a 1 cm (½ inch) border around the edge of each pastry square. Arrange the bananas, cut-side up, on the pastry inside the border, then brush the border with the beaten egg. Sprinkle the top of the bananas with the sugar.

Bake in a preheated oven, 200°C (400°F), Gas Mark 6, for 15–20 minutes or until the pastry is puffed and golden and the bananas are caramelized. Serve the tart hot with cream.

For cinnamon coffee liqueur cream as an alternative accompaniment to the tart, in a bowl whip 200 ml (7 fl oz) double cream until soft peaks form, then stir in 2 teaspoons ground cinnamon and 2 tablespoons Bailey's Irish Cream or any other creamy coffee liqueur.

date chocolate torte

Serves **4**
Preparation time **10 minutes**,
  plus cooling
Cooking time **30 minutes**

100 g (3½ oz) **flaked
  almonds**
125 g (4 oz) **plain dark
  chocolate**, roughly chopped
125 g (4 oz) **dried ready-to-
  eat dates**, pitted
3 **egg whites**
125 g (4 oz) **caster sugar**,
  plus 2 tablespoons for the
  topping
125 ml (4 fl oz) **whipping
  cream**
cocoa powder, to sprinkle

Grease a 23 cm (9 inch) springform tin and line with
nonstick baking paper. Put the almonds and chocolate
in a food processor and pulse until finely chopped.
Finely chop the dates with a knife.

Whisk the egg whites in a large, perfectly clean bowl
until soft peaks form. Slowly add the 125 g (4 oz)
sugar and continue whisking until it has dissolved.
Fold in the almond and chocolate mixture, then the
dates. Spoon the mixture into the prepared tin and
level the surface.

Bake in a preheated oven, 180°C (350°F), Gas Mark
4, for 30 minutes or until set and starting to come
away from the side. Leave to cool in the tin before
carefully turning out on to a serving plate.

Whip the cream and the remaining 2 tablespoons
sugar in a small bowl until soft peaks form. Using a
spatula, spread the cream evenly over the top of the
torte. Serve cut into thin slices and dusted with cocoa.

For iced date chocolate muffins, spoon the
chocolate mixture into 12 large, deep muffin tins lined
with paper cases and bake in a preheated oven,
180°C (350°F), Gas Mark 4, for 20–25 minutes or
until set. Transfer to a wire rack to cool. Melt 75 g
(3 oz) chopped plain dark chocolate with 40 g
(1½ oz) butter in a heatproof bowl set over a
saucepan of gently simmering water. Meanwhile,
toast 4 tablespoons flaked almonds in a dry frying
pan, stirring constantly, until golden brown. Stir the
chocolate mixture, then spoon over the muffins and
sprinkle with the toasted almonds. Leave until set.

madeleines

Makes **14**
Preparation time **15 minutes,**
  plus cooling
Cooking time **12 minutes**

3 **eggs**
100 g (3½ oz) **caster sugar**
150 g (5 oz) **plain flour**
100 g (3½ oz) **unsalted
  butter**, melted
grated rind of 1 **lemon**
grated rind of 1 **orange**

Brush a tray of madeleine moulds with melted butter and coat with plain flour, then tap the tray to remove the excess flour.

Whisk the eggs and sugar in a bowl until thick and pale and the whisk leaves a trail when lifted. Sift the flour, then gently fold into the egg mixture. Fold in the melted butter and lemon and orange rinds. Spoon into the moulds, leaving a little room for rising.

Bake in a preheated oven, 200°C (400°F), Gas Mark 6, for 12 minutes or until golden and springy to the touch. Remove the madeleines from the tray and leave to cool on a wire rack.

For quick sherry trifle, line the base of a dessert or trifle bowl with the madeleines and sprinkle over 2–3 tablespoons sweet sherry. Top with 300 g (10 oz) defrosted frozen mixed berries and top that with 200 ml (7 fl oz) custard. Whip 200 g (7 oz) double cream until soft peaks form and pipe or spoon over the top. Cover and chill in the refrigerator for 2–3 hours before serving.

coconut syllabub & almond brittle

Serves **4**
Preparation time **15 minutes**,
   plus cooling and chilling
Cooking time **about**
   10 minutes

100 g (3½ oz) **granulated**
   sugar
50 g (2 oz) **flaked almonds**,
   toasted

For the syllabub
200 ml (7 fl oz) **coconut**
   cream
300 ml (½ pint) **double cream**
15 **cardamom seeds**, lightly
   crushed
2 tablespoons **caster sugar**

To make the brittle, put the granulated sugar and almonds in a saucepan over a low heat. While the sugar melts, lightly oil a baking sheet. When the sugar has melted and turned golden, pour the mixture on to the baking sheet and leave to cool.

To make the syllabub, pour the coconut cream and double cream into a large bowl. Add the crushed cardamom seeds and caster sugar, then lightly whip until just holding soft peaks.

Spoon the syllabub into 4 glasses and chill in the refrigerator. Meanwhile, lightly crack the brittle into irregular shards. When ready to serve, top the syllabub with some of the brittle and serve the remainder separately on the side.

For lemon syllabub, put the grated rind and juice of 1 lemon in a bowl with 125 ml (4 fl oz) white wine and 40 g (1½ oz) caster sugar. Cover and leave to soak for about 1 hour. Whip 300 ml (½ pint) double cream until it forms soft peaks, then gradually add the wine mixture and continue whipping until it holds its shape. In a separate, perfectly clean bowl, whisk 1 egg white until stiff, then whisk in 40 g (1½ oz) caster sugar. Carefully fold into the cream mixture and spoon into 4 glasses. Chill in the refrigerator before serving.

lemon cookies

Makes **18–20**
Preparation time **15 minutes,**
  plus cooling
Cooking time **15–20 minutes**

125 g (4 oz) **unsalted butter,**
  diced and softened
125 g (4 oz) **caster sugar**
2 **egg yolks**
2 teaspoons grated
  lemon rind
150 g (5 oz) **plain flour**
100 g (3½ oz) **coarse**
  cornmeal
saffron, to sprinkle (optional)
icing sugar, for dusting

Line a baking sheet with nonstick baking paper. In a bowl, beat the butter and sugar together until light and fluffy. Mix in the egg yolks, lemon rind, flour and cornmeal until a soft dough forms.

Roll out the dough on a lightly floured surface to 1 cm (½ inch) thick. Using a 6 cm (2½ inch) round cutter, cut out rounds from the dough, re-rolling the trimmings. Transfer to the prepared baking sheet, then sprinkle with saffron, if liked, and bake in a preheated oven, 160°C (325°F), Gas Mark 3, for 15–20 minutes or until lightly golden. Transfer to a wire rack to cool, then dust with icing sugar.

For no-cook lemon cheesecakes, roughly crush 10 of the above biscuits and place them in the base of 4 dessert bowls or glasses. Whisk together 300 g (10 oz) cream cheese with the finely grated zest and juice of 1 lemon, 150 g (5 oz) caster sugar and 150 ml (¼ pint) double cream. Spoon this mixture into the prepared glasses and chill for 1–2 hours before serving.

lemon & orange mousse

Serves **4**
Preparation time **15 minutes**,
   plus chilling

300 ml (½ pint) **double cream**
grated rind and juice of
   1 **lemon**, plus extra finely
   pared strips of rind
   to decorate
grated rind and juice of
   ½ **orange**, plus extra finely
   pared strips of rind
   to decorate
65 g (2½ oz) **caster sugar**
2 **egg whites**

Whip together the cream, grated lemon and orange rinds and sugar in a large bowl until the mixture starts to thicken. Add the lemon and orange juices and whisk again until the mixture thickens.

Whip, in a separate large, perfectly clean bowl, the egg whites until soft peaks form, then fold into the citrus mixture. Spoon the mousse into 4 glasses and chill in the refrigerator. Decorate with lemon and orange rind strips.

For raspberry mousse, purée 200 g (7 oz) raspberries in a food processor or blender, then pass through a fine sieve. In a large bowl, whip together the cream and sugar as above until the mixture starts to thicken, then add the sieved raspberry purée and whip again until thickened. Continue with the recipe as above, but decorate with whole raspberries and plain dark chocolate shavings, shaved from a bar using a swivel-bladed vegetable peeler.

mango & passion fruit fool

Serves **4**
Preparation time **15 minutes**,
  plus chilling

2 ripe **mangoes**, peeled
  and stoned
1 tablespoon chopped **mint**
juice of ½ **lime**
250 ml (8 fl oz) **double cream**
250 ml (8 fl oz) **Greek yogurt**
2 **passion fruit**

Dice 1 mango and combine with the mint. Divide almost half the mango mixture between 4 small bowls, reserving a little for the topping.

Purée the remaining mango with the lime juice in a food processor or blender.

Beat the cream in a bowl until just holding soft peaks, then stir in the yogurt. Fold the cream mixture into the mango purée and swirl to marble.

Divide the cream mixture between the bowls and top with the reserved diced mango. Halve each passion fruit, then scoop the seeds of each half over each fool. Chill in the refrigerator until ready to serve.

For peach & amaretti fool, use a 400 g (13 oz) can peach halves, drained and diced, in place of the mango, mix with 2 tablespoons toasted flaked almonds and divide between 4 small bowls. Follow the recipe as above until the final stage. Then omit the passion fruit and instead top each dessert with a roughly crushed amaretti biscuit.

chocolate soufflés

Serves **4**
Preparation time **12 minutes**
Cooking time **about 15 minutes**

200 g (7 oz) **plain dark chocolate**, chopped
150 g (5 oz) **butter**, diced and softened
6 **eggs**
175 g (6 oz) **caster sugar**
125 g (4 oz) **plain flour**
icing sugar, to dust

Butter 4 x 200 ml (7 fl oz) ramekins. Melt the chocolate with the butter in a heatproof bowl set over a saucepan of gently simmering water.

Beat the eggs and sugar together in a bowl until very light and creamy. Sift the flour, then fold into the egg mixture. Fold in the chocolate mixture.

Divide the soufflé mixture between the prepared ramekins. Bake in a preheated oven, 180°C (350°F), Gas Mark 4, for 8–12 minutes. The soufflés should rise and form a firm crust, but you want them still to be slightly runny in the centre. Serve immediately dusted with icing sugar, with ice cream or cream.

For homemade vanilla ice cream to serve with the soufflés, in a heatproof bowl, mix together 1 whole egg, 1 egg yolk and 40 g (1½ oz) caster sugar. Bring 250 ml (8 fl oz) single cream gently to boiling point in a saucepan and pour on to the egg mixture, stirring vigorously. Strain, then stir in 1–2 drops vanilla extract. Leave to cool, then fold in 150 ml (¼ pint) whipped double cream. Pour into a rigid freezerproof container. Cover, seal and freeze for 1 hour. Remove and stir well, then re-freeze until firm. Transfer to the refrigerator 20 minutes before serving to soften.

peach & raspberry tartlets

Serves **4**
Preparation time **15 minutes**
Cooking time **8–10 minutes**,
  plus cooling

15 g (½ oz) **butter**, melted
4 sheets of **filo pastry**, each
  about 25 cm (10 inches)
  square
125 ml (4 fl oz) **double cream**
1 tablespoon **soft light
  brown sugar**
2 **peaches**, peeled, halved,
  stoned and diced
50 g (2 oz) **raspberries**
icing sugar, for dusting

Brush 4 deep muffin tins with the melted butter. Cut a sheet of filo pastry in half, then across into 4 equal-sized squares. Use these filo squares to line 1 muffin tin, arranging at slightly different angles, pressing down well and tucking the pastry into the tin neatly. Repeat with the remaining pastry to line the other muffin tins.

Bake the filo pastry tartlets in a preheated oven, 190°C (375°F), Gas Mark 5, for 8–10 minutes or until golden. Carefully remove the tartlet cases from the tins and leave to cool on a wire rack.

Whip the cream and brown sugar lightly in a bowl, until it holds its shape. Spoon into the tartlet cases and top with the peaches and raspberries. Dust with icing sugar. Serve immediately.

For strawberry and blueberry tartlets, grease 4 deep muffin tins as above. From ready-rolled shortcrust pastry (defrosted if frozen), cut out 4 rounds large enough to line the muffin tins. Prick the bases all over with a fork. Bake in a preheated oven, 190°C (375°F), Gas Mark 5, for 15 minutes or until golden brown. Carefully remove from the tins and leave to cool on a wire rack. Lightly whip the cream with 1 tablespoon icing sugar, then spoon into the tartlet cases. Top with 50 g (2 oz) sliced strawberries and 50 g (2 oz) blueberries. Dust with icing sugar and serve immediately.

index

acknowledgements

Executive Editor: Nicola Hill
Editor: Ruth Wiseall
Executive Art Editor: Leigh Jones
Designer: Jo Tapper
Photographer: Stephen Conroy
Home Economist: Sunil Vijayaker
Props Stylist: Liz Hippisley
Production Manager: Carolin Stransky

Special Photography: © Octopus Publishing Group Limited/Stephen Conroy
Other Photography: © Octopus Publishing Group Limited/Frank Adam 57, 127; /Neil Mersh 18, 24, 30, 44, 61, 73, 77, 79, 85, 103, 109, 131, 139, 142, 171, 174, 179 182, 189, 196, 203, 207, 213, 225, 235; /William Reavell 97; /Gareth Sambridge 135.